Succ

D0253145

Hanging Baskets and Containers

MARTIN WEIMAR

Series Editor:
LESLEY YOUNG

MEREHURST

Introduction

Contents

Have you ever thought of making a change from plain old boring red and pink pelargoniums on your balcony or in your windowbox? It is perfectly simple to ring the changes with plants and flowers in all shapes and colours, framed by lively shades of green – not just in summer but at any time of year! A huge number of enchanting plants are just waiting to be combined in many new ways so that they can flower in boxes, bowls, pots or hanging containers from spring right through to winter.

This guide to using hanging plants and baskets uses colour photographs to illustrate planting examples for the spring, summer, autumn and winter – all designed specially for this publication by author Martin Weimar. Here you will find an enormous variety of the most popular balcony plants, plus many new and rare ones. At-a-glance shopping lists and step-by-step instructions for planting and care make it easy for even the inexperienced gardener to create wonderful planting combinations.

If you wish to be adventurous and create your own planting arrangements you will find many basic tips on design, a guide to colour combinations and notes on the care of the most popular balcony plants.

This volume also contains basic information about buying, care, overwintering, propagating and pest control to ensure that your container-gardening ventures will be successful and trouble-free.

Morning glory (Ipomoea tricolor).

A red and white petunia hybrid.

Petunias, daisies, Swan River daisy and convolvulus.

The author
Martin Weimar is a gardener and flower artist who has exhibited his work in numerous art exhibitions. For many years he has run courses for people wishing to learn about the artistic arrangement of plants.

NB: Please read the Author's note on page 63.

Advice before planting

Every year flowering plants seem to invade more windows, balconies and patios, displayed in evermore beautiful containers and pouring from boxes and hanging baskets in a mass of flowers. In the following pages you will find all the information you need to know about balcony plants and where they come from, plus tips on buying, basic knowledge about containers and how to secure them, as well as several most important points about balconies themselves. If you take the prevailing conditions of light, rain and wind on your balcony into consideration when you choose your plants, you will be rewarded with luxuriant growth and a profusion of colourful blooms.

Shades of red for warm summer days
Semi-hanging and standard fuchsias (background) with Nierembergia (white and violet, centre) and Centradenia (pink, right) flourishing in a summer balcony box.

5

What are balcony plants?

The days of restricting one's balcony to the cultivation of pelargoniums and petunias in pots and containers have long passed. A multitude of annuals, perennials and shrubs, hitherto mostly only grown in gardens, has begun to appear in pots, troughs and boxes on our balconies.

The classic balcony plants

These small-flowering wonders will produce an endless array of flowers all summer long. They are not hardy and at the end of the season – depending on their length of life – are either placed in winter quarters or thrown away. The use of these plants can transform your balcony into a colour-rich paradise. The most important continuous-flowering plants are pelargoniums, fuchsias, begonias, busy lizzies, daisies, calceolaria and petunias.

A frothy profusion of blossom and robust good health are characteristics of most of the "new" balcony plants whose popularity has been rising steadily over the last few years:

● *Asteriscus maritimus*, golden yellow
● *Centradinia* "Cascade", red violet
● *Scaevola aemula*, violet
● convolvulus, *Convolulus sabatius*, light blue
● fleabane, *Erigeron karvinskianus*, white pink
● lobelia, *Lobelia erinus* "Richardii", light blue

Popular garden plants in containers

You will not obtain a continuous, summer-long display of flowers with these plants. Instead, your balcony will change with the seasons, allowing you to watch and appreciate the sequence of germination, flowering, fading and so on through the year, and thus enable you to enjoy the beauty of a much larger garden. Annual flowers and grasses, and even perennials and bulbous plants, will display their full charm over the seasons and will provide countless opportunities for surprising and unexpected nature study. When purchasing plants, give some thought to plants with interesting or beautiful seedheads (like grasses) and interesting colouring or berries in the autumn (like *Cotoneaster*). Woody perennials, grasses and shrubs are lovely to look at when covered with frost in winter. Do not forget that vegetables (such as tomatoes and lettuces), fruit (such as strawberries) or herbs and aromatic plants, which can enhance your culinary efforts, are easily grown on a balcony.

My tip: Be creative and use your imagination when arranging plants. Don't be afraid to try something new as such a wide range of flowering plants is available these days. Basically, plants with shallow roots are more suitable for growing in containers than plants with long, deep-growing roots. Many long-established and popular garden plants have now been improved by raisers to make them more suitable for balconies. The skill of such professional growers has produced varieties which are better able to stand the artificial climate of a town balcony. These cultivars do not mind so much if they have to survive briefly without water and are usually fairly resistant to pests and diseases. A great number of flowers, vegetables and woody plants have also been specially raised for growing in pots on balconies.

The history of balcony plants

Very early tomb decoration from ancient Egypt shows plants and flowers being cultivated in pots for use in the home or as part of religious ceremonies.

Plants grown in clay containers were used to decorate the courtyard gardens of the Egyptians and Greeks and later the Romans. Although balconies and loggias existed in Roman villas long before the birth of Christ, they were never decorated with living plants. The balconies of the nobility were usually sited in an exposed position and although often splendidly decorated with flower garlands, these were made of mortar or plaster and served solely as a symbol of the political allegiance of their owners well into the nineteenth century.

It was not until drastic changes came about in society, together with the expansion of cities and the beginning of the construction of blocks of rented accommodation in the last century, that flowers and woody plants began to appear on balconies. This development was supported by the importation of many new plant discoveries from overseas. Soon such new plants began to reach Europe in ever-increasing numbers.

● Around 1700, the early forms of pelargoniums were brought from South Africa to the Netherlands.
● Around 1800, the culture of fuchsias in gardens began.
● In 1822, calceolaria (*Calceolaria integrifolia*) was brought to Europe from Chile.
● In 1849, the first double petunia (a cultivar) came on to the market.
● In 1880, a plant-hunting expedition brought back busy lizzies from Zanzibar.

Ancestry and origins

The plants which flower for us year after year on our balconies are guests from many different countries. A large proportion of summer-flowering plants hail from subtropical and tropical regions.

Balcony plants from the tropics

These plants are not restricted to an annual cycle of growth that depends on temperature and light and therefore flower profusely all year round. They do not need a rest period and will even continue to flower quite happily in their winter quarters. They grow best in high temperatures and high humidity and will require rather a lot of fertilizer, e.g. busy lizzies, whose ancestors derive from tropical East Africa, Sri Lanka, India and New Guinea.

Balcony plants from the subtropics

These plants will only produce an abundance of flowers during the summer months. Their growth is characterized by an extreme alter-nation of rainy and dry periods. When rain does fall in their coun-tries of origin, these plants germi-nate and flower very rapidly. As soon as the next dry period sets in, they quickly form seeds. You can delay the end of the flowering per-iod and subsequent seed formation by giving them plenty of water. One such example is the Cape marigold (*Dimorphotheca sinuata*) which originates from South Africa. Other plants from this climatic zone have the ability to store water. They can be recognized by their fleshy leaves and stalks, e.g. *Scaevola aemula.* - Forget-me-not

Fuchsia hybrid "Avelanche".

Length of life

Plants are divided into three different groups, depending on their natural, biologically programmed length of life.

Annual plants germinate, flower, form seeds and die down during the course of one year (e.g. zinnias, cornflowers, China asters). They cannot be overwintered and have to be grown from seed every year.

Biennials are plants which are sown out in the second/third month of summer and which will germinate and grow leaves in the same year. Their main flowering time, however, is during the following spring or summer. Biennials which flower in the spring (like pansies, wallflowers, forget-me-nots) are particularly suited to growing in pots. After withering, they can be replaced by summer-flowering plants.

Perennials are woody herbaceous plants and shrubs and also bulbous plants. With the proper care and correct overwintering, they can go on growing for many years. Depending on their origins, they may be hardy and can be overwintered outside (with some form of protection if grown in small containers, see p. 52). Others have to be protected from the cold and overwintered indoors. Many of our balcony plants are tropical or subtropical perennials, which means that they grow for several years in their countries of origin. However, when they are grown in a temperate climate, overwintering them indoors tends to create more work than simply resowing them every spring.

Bursting with colour
Alpine balconies and windowboxes are famous worldwide for their profusions of bright, colourful flowers.

For this reason, they are often grown as annuals in the northern hemisphere.

Hardy perennials, on the other hand, can overwinter outside if given some protection (see p. 52). The leafy, above-ground parts of these plants are not hardy and die off in the winter. However, the plant will survive the cold season as underground tubers, rootstocks or rhizomes, from which it produces new shoots in the spring.

Buying plants or growing your own

Balcony plants can be bought as ready-grown, flowering plants or as not-yet-flowering, small, young plants. The alternative is to grow them yourself. Whichever you decide to do, both ways have their pros and cons.

Buying flowering plants

It is most exciting to stroll around a garden centre or street market on a sunny morning after the long, grey days of winter and take home a slection of colourful spring plants for the first decoration of your balcony. The purchase of ready-to-plant flowering plants is always bound up with a feeling of optimistic anticipation.

Advantages
● Flowering plants are ideal for a quick planting without much preparation.
● You will save time, effort and space which would otherwise be taken up with the sowing and cultivation of seedlings and young plants.
● You can enjoy lovely flowering plants nearly all year round on your balcony. The great selection offered by nurseries and garden centres at any time of the year makes this quite possible.

● The wide range of plants available means that you do not have to imagine the future "look" of your balcony. When purchasing grown plants you will be able to combine your chosen species in the colours you desire from the selection offered for sale.

Disadvantages
● Flowering balcony plants are more expensive than young plants or seeds, while transporting bushy, flowering plants is riskier than moving small ones about.
● Most flowering plants suitable for a summer balcony are on sale by the middle of the second month of spring. In regions with a less clement climate, most of these plants cannot tolerate being placed outside until about the middle of the third month of spring. If you wish to choose from a large selection, however, you have to buy early and make sure the plants have a bright, sheltered position and plenty of care.

Buying young plants

Young plants are rooted cuttings (e.g. pelargoniums) or pricked out seedlings (e.g. annual summer flowers or vegetables).

Advantages
● Young plants are considerably cheaper than plants in flower. You may even occasionally get a discount if you buy large quantities.
● Young plants root better than plants in flower as they are still in the vegetative phase of their growth.

Disadvantage
● Young plants are often for sale long before the correct time to plant them out. This means that you need space and will have to invest time in their further cultivation. You can continue to cultivate plants that are sensitive to frost on a windowsill, in a greenhouse or in a cold frame.

Growing your own balcony plants

If you want to grow rare annuals or biennials on your balcony, you will probably have to cultivate your own plants. Usually, you will have to obtain seeds or bulbs from specialist mail order firms or nurseries. Perennials and shrubs take many years to grow into good-looking plants. It is best to leave the growing of them to nurseries etc. and invest in the purchase of larger specimens.

Advantages of sowing seed

● Growing your own balcony plants from seed is cheaper.
● It can be quite an exciting experience, especially for children.
● The sowing of fast-germinating summer flower seeds is particulary problem-free; they can be sown outside in balcony boxes without special protection from the end of the second month of spring onwards.
● The planting of bulbs in the autumn is equally simple. They can be overwintered in their containers outside (see p. 22).

Disadvantages

● Patience, time, a little discipline in care and an understanding of basic gardening principles are necessary for success.
● In particular, the early cultivation of frost-sensitive balcony flowers may entail great cost and work. Depending on the extent to which you wish to cultivate your own plants, you will require either a large preserving jar or a mini-propagator with automatic climate control. Very often you will have access to at least one warm windowsill where you can germinate seeds, but you may well lack a cool, very bright position indoors which the plants require at a later stage. This may result in the young plants shooting too fast, growing lanky, falling over and decaying before they can be

Buying through the year

Spring-flowering plants: Buy and plant bulbs in the first to second months of autumn.

Summer flowers

● Plants in flower can be bought from the second month of spring; young plants from the first month of spring.
● Seeds of annuals are sown between the last month of winter and the second month of spring, depending on cultivation times.
● Seeds of biennials are best sown during the second and third months of summer of the preceding year. Biennials can also be bought as young plants.
● Buy perennials as young plants in the spring.

Autumn flowers: Perennials which bloom in the autumn should be bought as young plants the previous spring or in the summer as large, individual plants. Asters, chrysanthemums and *Erica* are obtainable in flower from late summer/early autumn.

Winter planting: Evergreen woody plants or winter-flowering shrubs etc. can be planted from spring onwards or in the autumn.

taken outside after late frosts are over.

Where to buy plants

The best place to buy plants is in nurseries which grow their own balcony plants. Garden centres, weekly markets and flower shops also offer a wide range of plants which are usually of good quality and accompanied by a tag offering advice on care. Be careful when buying plants in supermarkets etc. Such plants may be attractively priced but their quality may leave

much to be desired, particularly if they have been stored in unfavourable conditions on shelves in a large warehouse etc. Very rare flowers will have to be grown from seed or bulbs which can only be obtained from specialist mail order firms and nurseries.

The right position

Before buying any plants, you should take a good long look at the balcony or window that you are intending to use. The health and development of plants depends greatly on the availability of water and nutrients but also on the position in which the plants are kept. The influence of light, temperature, wind and rain is very important too and these four key factors are required to varying degrees by different plants. Fuchsias, for example, do not like the bright sunlight of a south-facing position; pelargoniums and petunias, on the other hand, will become sickly and die if exposed to too much rain. This means that you will need to find out the exact requirements of the plants you would like to grow before you buy any of them. Ask yourself the following questions with respect to the position you are able to offer:
● Which direction does the position face? (See position of the balcony, p. 11.)
● Is the position sheltered from wind and rain? (See p. 12.)
● How much light will they receive? (See sun, shade, semi-shade, p. 12.)
● Will the full-grown weight of the plants be suitable for the weight-carrying capacity of the balcony; will they grow too tall in front of a window?
Considering these points will help you to avoid making mistakes and wasting money.

Strawberries will produce a rich harvest of fruit in a container if fertilized properly.

The position of the balcony

The light and temperature conditions on a balcony (and also in front of a window) are dependent on the direction it is facing and on the height and proximity of the surrounding buildings.

A south-facing balcony will provide sunlight throughout the entire day. During the summer this will also mean plenty of heat. Sensitive plants may get burnt in such a position. In any case, plenty of watering is important. South-east- and south-west-facing positions are optimal, as all plants, apart from those which love shade, will thrive.

A north-facing balcony is always in shade as direct sunlight will never penetrate it. As there will not be enough sun to dry up accumulated rain and excess water from watering, moisture will often be retained in the compost over considerable periods of time. Only a very few balcony plants will thrive here.

East- or west-facing balconies have similar light conditions. Neither is subjected to intense, bright, midday sunlight. An east-facing balcony will receive the softer sunlight of the morning. A west-facing balcony benefits from the afternoon and evening sun but this often also means greater exposure to the weather, including storms and rain.

My tip: A south-facing balcony may actually benefit from being roofed over or having a tree growing in front of it to provide some shade. On the other hand, a white house wall opposite a north-facing balcony may reflect the sunlight and make the balcony much lighter than normal.

○ = **sun**: This plant needs, and copes well with, plenty of sunlight. A south-facing position is very important for the development of flowers.

● = **shade**: The plant copes well with, or likes, shade and can even be planted in a north-facing position.

◑ = **semi-shade**: The plant will thrive best in a bright position that is not exposed to harsh midday sunlight. This is to be found in east- or south-east-facing positions, as well as in west- or south-west-facing positions.

Containers

All balcony plants gain by being planted in an attractive container that complements the plant itself and goes well with the surroundings. The gardening trade has on offer a huge selection of different pots, large containers, boxes, bowls, troughs, hanging containers and amphorae made of various materials. When buying any containers, consider the following points when choosing, checking and comparing them: material, shape, size, weight, durability and price.

Every good plant container should have:

● enough room so that the plant will have sufficient compost and space to develop its rooting system. This is particularly important for plants which are intended to last longer than just one summer. If the plant pot is too small, the plant may not receive enough water during the summer as there will be barely enough moisture-storing compost in the pot;

● drainage holes for excess water, so that no waterlogging can occur, causing root decay if the plants are watered too much or if they are left

Espaliers provide privacy and protection from the wind.

Wind and rain

West-facing positions are often subject to unprotected exposure to wind and rain. Further, do remember that sensitive plants might snap or be bent over on rooftop gardens, balconies situated in elevated positions or exposed patios. Some warmth-loving balcony plants will not thrive if they are subjected to showers of rain.

Sun, shade, semi-shade

These terms are used by nurseries and garden centres to describe the light requirements of plants. Generally, the following symbols are used in any brief information on care.

standing out in the rain;
● frost resistance if you wish to overwinter hardy plants like conifers, small deciduous trees or shrubs outside.

My tip: Every time you buy a pot or container, also buy a matching dish or saucer to go underneath to catch excess water. This will prevent unsightly water marks and moss rings on the balcony floor and complaints from neighbours.

Different materials

Plastic containers: Containers made of plastic are weather-resistant, light in weight and generally inexpensive to buy. During the summer, they keep the compost moist longer than clay post as the walls of the container do not absorb any moisture and no water evaporates through them either.
Disadvantages: plastic containers are not particularly attractive. In south-facing positions, they may even heat up so much that the roots are damaged.
Terracotta containers are beautiful and complement all plants. They come in very simple styles or with lots of ornamentation. They are stable and their porous walls allow the plants' roots to breathe. On the other hand, during the summer a lot of moisture is lost through evaporation. Disadvantages: they are expensive, break if dropped and are often not resistant to frost.
Concrete composite containers can now be bought which do not contain asbestos. They are heavy, therefore stable, frost-proof and allow the roots of plants to breathe. They can be painted any colour. Disadvantages: they are expensive and tend to crack at the least knock.
Wooden containers: are of medium weight and frost-resistant. Disadvantages: they are expensive

Health and safety on your balcony

If you live in rented accommodation, you probably may, in principle, use your balcony freely for your own purposes providing you do not infringe upon the rights of other tenants or the landlord. Many rental agreements do not allow tenants to hang balcony boxes on the outside of a balcony.
● Generally, a tenant may place balcony boxes on a balcony without the landlord's permission and plant them in any way he/she likes. The limits to these rights are defined by not using anything which might endanger the stability of the balcony railing or detract from the appearance of the exterior of the house.
● If you want lots of balcony boxes or to use a heavy, large container for plants, you will have to check the carrying capacity and design of the balcony beforehand.
● Check first with your landlord (in writing) whether any structural changes can be made to the balcony, such as the fixing of espaliers, balcony cladding or painting the balcony wall or floor with any kind of paint, etc. Apartment owner-occupiers should check with their neighbours. Even if you do have written

consent, these structural changes will probably have to be removed again when the term of rental expires if your landlord so wishes.
● Make sure that you secure balcony boxes in such a way that they cannot be blown down by wind or storms (see pp. 14/15). Many boxes bought in the trade are equipped with a "safety lip" (see illustration, p. 14) to prevent the box from tipping.
● Check the safety of the fixtures at regular intervals.
● Do not allow water to run or drip down the façade of the house or on to a neighbour's balcony. Particularly in the autumn and winter, water can become a source of danger if it happens to run down on to the pavement and then freezes. Always place a saucer under each container.
● Only spray with plant protection agents when your neighbours are not on their balcony. Make sure that the spray never drifts on to a neighbouring balcony.

and need a lot of care. They are susceptible to damp and have to be treated with plant-friendly wood preserver quite regularly. Always stand them on wooden blocks or bricks for better ventilation.

Care of containers

Clay pots or containers should always be thoroughly soaked in water before use. Very large clay pots can be left in the rain for several days or hosed down with a gar-

den hose for a while. After plants have been removed from pots, the pots should be scrubbed thoroughly with a brush under running water. Chalk deposits on terracotta containers can be left as they endow them with a certain sought-after patina. Put all containers which are not frost-proof in a sheltered position before the first frosts begin.

Securing containers

Balcony boxes, pots and hanging containers should be secured safely, firmly and sensibly so that they will stand up to rough or stormy weather. Unsecured containers are a danger to pedestrians and passersby and may be the cause of injuries or damage.

NB: Always provide containers with saucers to catch excess water!

Securing hanging containers

The space on a balcony is always limited and hanging containers provide an excellent way of accommodating more plants. Hanging containers are usually suspended in a sheltered position on a jutting piece of wall or from a ceiling by means of a hook and dowel. They should hang high enough so that you do not bump into them and the growth of the plant should not be hampered by lack of height. Give some careful thought to the spot from which you are planning to hang the container. As enchanting as hanging containers look, particularly if they are secured high enough, they are often given less care for this very reason. Watering, tidying and infestation with pests are often forgotten about or neglected. There are a number of ways of securing hanging containers, which will make these jobs easier.

Securing a container with a pulley:

The hanging container is not secured by means of a hook but is attached to a roller or wheel by means of a longish chain running down the side wall to a point where it is secured. All necessary plant care can be undertaken by lowering the hanging container by releasing the chain and then pulling it up again later on. This sensible device

can be obtained in the gardening trade.

Wall-mounted anchoring (see illustration 1): Hanging containers which are secured to a side wall by means of wall-mounted fixtures are easy to reach. You will find many types of attractive wrought-iron fixtures in the gardening trade.

My tip: Ropes made of natural fibres are very attractive but do make sure that the weight-carrying parts of the rope do not come into contact with damp compost. The constant dampness will rot the rope and the hanging container could come crashing down. Chains, wire-and-plastic rope and galvanized wire are safer.

Securing balcony boxes

Depending on the architectural design of your balcony, you will be able to fit balcony box fixtures and fastenings bought from gardening centres etc. by yourself without much trouble. Make sure to find out beforehand whether the railing is able to support the weight of heavy

1 A wrought-iron wall bracket for a hanging container.

balcony boxes and whether you are permitted to hang them from the railing. Very often, you will find that hanging them on the outside of the balcony is not permitted.

2 A standard balcony box fixture for hanging containers inside and outside a railing. 3 Secure metal corners for screwing on to balustrades with a protruding lip. 4 Metal straps for securing wooden boxes to wooden railings.

Special balcony fixtures for boxes (see illustration 2): Balcony boxes can be hung on both the inside and the outside of a balcony railing. These fixtures can be adjusted to suit the width of the boxes and the railing by means of screws. Horizontal metal pieces can be placed across the boxes and screwed to the fixture to stop the boxes from tipping. Plastic boxes containing heavy plants tend to sag and should be placed on such supports at intervals of about 40 cm (16 in).

Balcony box fixtures (see illustration 3): These corner supports will enable you to stand balcony boxes safely on the tops of balcony railings and windowsills. They are screwed down and prevent the boxes from falling off.

Metal straps (see illustration 4): This is one of the simplest methods of securing wooden boxes to broad wooden railings. You will need metal pieces with holes in them – obtainable in all sizes from builders' suppliers and DIY centres. The boxes can be firmly attached to the railing by means of screws.

Safe positioning of individual pots

Individual flowerpots are even less stable than boxes. Despite this, they are still very popular for decorating window ledges, as they can be exchanged very easily without the need for replanting.

Securing flowerpots on a window ledge (see illustration 5): You can build a very simple but effective means of securing flowerpots using two angle irons and a strong wooden batten. The angle irons should be dowelled into the wall on either side of the window at about the height of the top edge of the pots. There should be no space left between the batten and the pots so that the pots will not be able to top-

5 Securing individual pots on a window ledge using a batten.

6 Individual flowerpots standing in a flower box under a window ledge.

ple over. The batten should be screwed to the angle irons.

Pots in flowerboxes (see illustration 6): This is a simple method of enlarging the standing space on a window ledge which is too narrow. Use dowels to secure balcony box holders to the wall below the window ledge. You can stand individual pots in such a securely fastened box and exchange them at any time. Naturally, this method is also suitable for securing individual pots to balcony railings, both inside and outside.

Securing individual pots to a balcony railing (see illustration 7): Wire holders for holding pots can be obtained in the trade. This is an attractive idea, especially for small balconies, and is a means of equipping even awkward corners with some greenery.

You will also be able to find pot holders that can be jammed inside the pot in order to attach it to the vertical bars of balcony railings. These simple aids can be obtained in many sizes and versions. Lots of plants can be attached in this way, to railings or even an espalier.

7 Fixtures for attaching individual pots to railings and corners.

My tip: Individual pots can also be secured in the following way. Push a length of galvanized wire in through the drainage hole of a pot and up through the compost until it appears at the top of the pot. Bend the two ends of wire until they meet and then attach the pot to a balcony railing by means of the wire.

15

Balcony boxes for all seasons

Delicate, fresh spring flowers, splendid summer plantings, golden red autumn colours and lively green in the middle of winter can all be achieved on any balcony without a lot of work or expense. Whether you have ample space or very little, most planting combinations will prove quite feasible, whether in a flower box, bowl, hanging container, pot or large container. The following pages will provide you with many ideas for planting designs as well as planting plans for the spring, summer, autumn and winter.

A planting of colourful summer flowers
All the splendour of summer is captured in this box. The red pelargoniums provide a cheerful splash of colour in between the yellow black-eyed Susan and marigolds surrounded by dark blue petunias and convolvulus (see p. 29).

Helpful tips for planting arrangements

The charm of your balcony garden will be considerably enhanced by a clever choice of plants, wise colour combinations and skilful grouping. Flowers that are harmoniously combined may actually complement and increase each other's individual charms.

Always consider the visual effect!

Anyone setting out to group plants together is aiming for enhanced surroundings and visual pleasure for themselves and others. Before buying and planting any plants, you should consider a few basic rules.

At a distance, a good effect can be obtained by using plants which have large flowers and/or flower profusely. For example, the multi-storied balconies of large farmhouses in the alpine regions of Europe are often bedecked with pelargoniums, petunias or begonias.

Close-up effect: If you intend to create a green oasis on a small balcony, primarily for your own viewing, you can choose plants with few, delicate-petalled flowers as these will be most effective when seen close up.

Surroundings: Be it against a concrete wall, a wooden railing or a wrought-iron railing, when any grouping of plants is placed in front of a background, they will influence the general effect colour-wise. It is better to place strong colours in front of a white wall. Dark backgrounds, on the other hand, contrast well with light, pastel-coloured flowers.

Optical balance: While arranging your plants, imagine that your balcony box is a see-saw with the centre of gravity right in the middle. Plants that are well balanced will look "right". This does not mean planting exactly the same on the left and right of the box. A tall plant on one side will require the planting of a counter-balance to the overall shape, e.g. the introduction of a hanging plant or bushy flower.

Formal plantings

This style follows different rules to those observed by a more natural design. By "formal" we mean the use of plants which are intended to beautify and decorate an entire balcony or house façade when viewed from the outside. Plants are placed for visual effect, i.e. standards or tall plants go into the background and low-growing, hanging or semi-hanging balcony plants are recommended for the foreground where they will drape gracefully over the edges of their containers.

My tip: Do not place flowers that grow too tall in front of windows as they will restrict the amount of light coming in through the window.

Natural-looking designs

Here, the usual arrangement of low-growing and tall plants is treated more casually. Sometimes tall plants will be placed in the foreground, while hanging or climbing plants may grow through other plants from the centre and smaller flowers may be hidden behind larger ones. When out for a walk, try to observe the way wild plants grow and where they occur. Nature does not arrange things in neat rows or according to height, but generally hides away little surprises, e.g. a small pocket of delicate little flowers may well be discovered hiding behind a sheltering bush.
For this reason, when you are choosing plants for natural planting designs, do not just go for straight-growing plants but also consider crooked ones or those that appear to grow to one side.

My tip: Do not be too keen to start snipping away with your secateurs; do this only if the luxuriant growth of one plant is beginning to smother a neighbouring plant.

Combining colours

A long, strung-out band of similarly coloured hanging pelargoniums is seen by human eyes as tranquil but, at the same time, it may also appear rather

An entire balcony decorated in blue.

boring. Make sure that there is variety among the colours you choose.
● Complementary colours make each other glow brilliantly. Red and green, blue and orange, yellow and violet have this effect.
● Several different shades of the same colour can be very elegant.
● Cool colours are blue, bluish-red, violet, blue green, greenish-yellow and white. All of these combine very well.
● Warm colours are yellow, orange, cinnebar red and yellow green. They also harmonize well.
● Of course, you can combine warm and cool colours but this will require more conscious care over your choice of shades.
Nothing should go wrong if you decide on one range of colours for your main scheme and use another range merely to provide an "accent". This can be done quite simply by distinguishing clearly between the ratios of colour quantities: many plants from one range (e.g. warm colours) with few from the other range (cool colours).
● Green is often forgotten when choosing balcony plants. It provides a quiet zone among the colourful flowers. Green is usually the colour of leaves but green tones can be enhanced by employing such interesting plants as asparagus, grasses or ivies. Green and white leaves, as in the popular *Plectranthus coleoides* or the variegated varieties of ivy, add light to the plant arrangement.

Notes on colour and care of the most common balcony plants

	Other flower colours	Also white	Botanical name / Common name	Flowering time	Position	Watering	Over-wintering
			Brachycome iberidifolia / **Swan River daisy**	esm-ma	○ ◐	watering can (outline)	house (outline)
	pink		*Convolvulus tricolor* / **dwarf convolvulus**	esm-ea	○ ◐	watering can (filled)	1 (filled)
			Convolvulus sabatius / **convolvulus**	lsp-ma	○ ◐	watering can (outline)	house (outline)
			Felicia amelloides	lsp-ma	○ ◐	watering can (outline)	house (outline)
			Heliotropium arborescens / **heliotrope** ☠	lsp-ma	○ ◐ rain-sensitive	watering can (filled)	house (outline)
	pink	✓	*Lobelia erinus* / **lobelia**	lsp-ma	○ ◐ ●	watering can (filled)	1 (filled)
	pink		*Alyssum maritimum* / **sweet alyssum**	lsp-ea	○ ◐	watering can (outline)	1 (filled)
	pink		*Myosotis sylvatica* / **forget-me-not**	msp-lsm	○ ◐	watering can (outline)	1 (filled)
			Scaevola aemula	esm-ma	○ ◐	watering can (outline)	house (outline)
	cream, yellow, orange, red, pink	✓	*Viola wittrockiana* hybrids / **pansies**	ea-esm	○ ◐	watering can (outline)	keyhole symbol
Cool colours: pink through purple	red	✓	*Bellis perennis* / **daisy**	lw-esm	○ ◐	watering can (filled)	keyhole symbol
	yellow, red, violet, blue		*Callistephus chinensis* / **China aster**	lsm-ma	○ ◐	watering can (outline)	1 (filled)
			Centradenia	esm-ma	○ ◐	watering can (outline)	house (outline)
	cream, yellow, orange, red, red brown, violet		*Chrysanthemum indicum* hybrids ☠	ea-la	○ ◐ ●	watering can (outline)	house (outline)
			Erigeron karvinskianus / **fleabane**	lsp-ma	○ ◐	watering can (outline)	house (outline)
	orange, violet, green		*Fuchsia* / **fuchsia**	lsp-ma	◐ ● wind-sheltered	watering can (filled)	house (outline)
	orange, red, violet		*Impatiens* hybrids / **busy lizzy**	lsp-ma	◐ ● rain-sensitive	watering can (outline)	house (outline)
	yellow, red, violet, blue	✓	*Petunia* hybrids / **petunia** ☠	lsp-ma	○ ◐ rain-sensitive	watering can (filled)	1 (filled)
	cream, yellow, orange, red		*Rosa* / **balcony rose**	esm-ma	○ ◐	watering can (outline)	keyhole symbol
	red, salmon pink, violet, blue		*Verbena* hybrids / **verbena**	lsp-ma	○ ◐	watering can (filled)	1 (filled)

Key to the symbols

If you wish to plant an entire flower box or even your whole balcony with your favourite colour, you will find suggestions here as well as an indication of the other colours in which each flower can be grown. White flowers are indicated in a separate column.

Flowering time

esp = early spring
msp = mid-spring
lsp = late spring
esm = early summer
msm = mid-summer
lsm = late summer
ea = early autumn
ma = mid-autumn
la = late autumn
ew = early winter
mw = mid-winter
lw= late winter

Position

○ sunny ◐ semi-shady ● shady

(rain-sensitive) The plant is sensitive to rain; protect from wetness.

(wind-sheltered) The plant requires a wind-sheltered position.

Notes on colour and care of the most common balcony plants

Warm colours: yellow through orange

Warm colours: red through red brown

Other flower colours	Also white	Botanical name / Common name	Flowering time	Position	Watering	Over-wintering
		Asteriscus maritimus	lsp-ma	○ ◐	medium	indoors
		Calceolaria integrifolia / calceolaria	lsp-ma	○ ◐	plentifully	annual
pink		*Chrysanthemum frutescens*	lsp-ma	○ ◐	medium	indoors
cream		*Dimorphotheca sinuata* / Cape marigold	lsp-ea	○ ◐	medium	annual
cream, red brown, brown		*Helianthus annuus* / sunflower	lsm-ma	○ ◐ ⇄	plentifully	annual
cream, pink, red, blue		*Nemesia* hybrids / nemesia	lsp-ea	○ ◐	medium	annual
		Sanvitalia procumbens	lsp-ma	○ ◐	medium	annual
		Thunbergia alata / black-eyed Susan	lsp-ma	○ ◐ ⇄	medium	annual
		Thymophylla tenuiloba	esm-ma	○ ◐	medium	annual
cream, red, red brown		*Tropaeolum* hybrids / nasturtium	lsp-ma	○ ◐ ●	plentifully	annual
yellow, orange, pink, salmon pink	☠	*Begonia* hybrids / tuber begonia	msp-ma	◐ ●	medium	indoors
yellow, orange, pink		*Cheiranthus cheiri* / wallflower	msp-esm	○	medium	outside with protection
pink, salmon pink		*Dianthus sinensis* hybrids / garden pink	esm-ma	○ ◐	medium	annual
pink		*Erica herbacea* / winter heather	ma-ew	○ ◐ ●	plentifully	annual
cream, yellow, orange, pink		*Gazania* hybrids / gazania	esm-ea	○	medium	indoors
yellow, orange, pink	☠	*Lantana camara* hybrids	lsp-ma	○ ◐	medium	indoors
cream, pink, green	☠	*Nicotiana sandere* / tobacco plant	lsp-ma	○ ◐ ●	medium	annual
pink, salmon pink, violet		*Pelargonium* / pelargonium	lsp-ma	○ ◐	plentifully	indoors
yellow, orange, pink, blue, violet	☠	*Primula vulgaris* hybrids / primula	mw-lsp	○ ◐	medium	outside with protection
yellow, orange	☠	*Tagetes* hybrids / tagetes	esm-ma	○ ◐	medium	annual

Watering:

- plentifully
- medium

Overwintering:

- **1** Annual, cannot be overwintered
- Needs to be overwintered indoors
- Can be overwintered outside with protection

Warning:

- ☠ The plant is toxic or contains skin-irritants

Ideas for spring

After a long, grey winter we yearn for bright colours and fresh shades of green. We look forward to seeing snowdrops, crocuses, tulips and narcissi. Remember to plant the bulbs in good time so that you can enjoy these cheerful harbingers of spring in all their colourful splendour.

Most spring flowers are bulbous plants which will only produce their fresh, delicate flowers if their particular germinating and growth programmes have been taken into account.

When to plant bulbs

In the autumn: All bulbous plants which flower in the spring and are required to withstand frosty winter nights should be planted in frost-resistant containers in the autumn. From late summer onwards, garden centres and nurseries offer a wide range of spring-flowering bulbs. Rare plants can be obtained from special mail order firms. When buying bulbs, remember to make sure that they have no mouldy patches and are not dried up. If you do not intend to plant them immediately after buying them, store the bulbs in a dark, cool place (on no account in plastic bags!) until they are to be planted.

How to plant bulbs: Plant the bulbs with the shoot tip pointing upwards and, if possible, set them in the soil or compost at a depth of twice their height. It is sometimes difficult to tell the top from the bottom in bulbs but, usually, the presence of dried-up little roots indicates the bottom. If you do happen to plant a bulb the wrong way up, it will not matter too much. The bulb will right itself but will probably take a little longer to flower.

Stand the plant containers in a sheltered corner of your balcony and keep the compost evenly moist so that the roots can develop. Do not forget your bulbs during the winter and remember to water them in frost-free, dry weather.

In the spring: You can save yourself the trouble of bringing on bulbs through the winter if you buy bulbous plants on the point of flowering in the spring. Nurseries will have done all the work in advance and often start selling the first spring-flowering plants from the middle of the first month of winter. However, these plants will have been cultivated under artificial conditions in high temperatures and would freeze to death outside in frosty weather. These plants are really only suitable for the short-term decoration of a balcony or living room. A long-term planting using pre-cultivated spring flowers should not be undertaken until the outside temperatures are definitely above freezing. You can extend the flowering time of such a planting if you:
● cover the plants with bubble pack, paper or cloths whenever the temperatures drop to around freezing;
● stand them in a semi-shady, that is not a sunny, position;
● stand them indoors in a cool, shady place.

What to do after the flowers have finished

If the bulbs are planted in large containers and are intended as permanent plantings, all you need to do is remove the dead flowers and brown leaves. Never cut off the green parts of bulbous plants. If you want them to flower again the following year, you will have to leave the plant to draw all the strength from the leaves back into the bulb. If you want to change the plants every season, it is not worth continuing to grow the bulbs nor storing them. It is much simpler and more successful to buy new bulbs each autumn. If you have a garden, you can remove the bulbs from their container and plant them out.

My tip: Plant pansies spaced evenly in your favourite colours in boxes and bowls in the autumn. Then add lots of different-coloured tulip bulbs at irregular intervals between them. Keep the compost moist during the winter and this arrangement will be transformed into a wild firework display of colourful tulips in the spring.

Spring on the balcony
Here you can catch the first warming rays of sun among overwintered plants and colourful spring flowers.

Ideas for the spring

There follow a few planting suggestions for those of you who like to do things spontaneously and fairly quickly. All of these cheerful spring flowers can be obtained in a pre-cultivated state, on the point of flowering or already flowering in early spring.

A primula box in warm shades

This involves very little work for maximum effect. These flowering plants appear for sale in the gardening trade as early as the beginning of the second month of winter.
Plants for a 60-cm (24 in) box:
12 primulas, *Primula vulgaris* hybrids
Planting and care: Plant the primulas at staggered intervals with those at the front leaning slightly over the edge of the box. Water well and fertilize once a week. If the temperature drops to around freezing, cover them with

newspaper. From the last month of spring, transplant them into the garden where they will flower again next year. The box can then be reused for summer planting.

Two small willows in a large container

Plants for a large container with a diameter of 50 cm (20 in):
2 small willows, *Salix caprea* "Pendula"
6 lesser periwinkles, *Vinca minor*
1 Christmas rose, *Helleborus* hybrid
1 pot of scented narcissi, *Narcissus tazetta* "Cheerfulness", (about 4 bulbs per pot)
2 pots of grape hyacinths, *Muscari aucheri* (about 5 bulbs per pot)
Planting and care: Buy the willow, periwinkles and Christmas rose in early spring. Place the Christmas rose in the front and plant periwinkles all around the remainder of the container.

Leave some space for the narcissi and grape hyacinths which you will not be able to buy until later on. Plant the narcissi in the background and the grape hyacinths near the stems of the willows. Stand the container in a semi-shady position and water and fertilize regularly. The lesser periwinkle

will flower from about the second to third month of spring. The container can be overwintered outside with some protection. Fertilize again the following year.

Warning: Christmas roses and narcissus bulbs are toxic!

Primulas make a good arrangement for any position.

Willows must be planted in a frost-proof container.

An Easter bowl in shades of violet

This is a decorative bowl for indoors, which may also be placed outside.
Plants for a bowl with a diameter of 25 cm (10 in):
2 primulas, *Primula vulgaris* hybrids
3 pots of grape hyacinths, *Muscari aucheri* (about 5 bulbs per pot)
3 hyacinths, *Hyacinthus orientalis* "Bismarck"
1 pot of glory of the snow, *Chionodoxa gigantea* (several bulbs per pot)
Planting and care: The plants can be obtained in flower from the second month of winter onwards. Plant them in an arrangement according to their height: set the primulas and glory of the snow in front, the grape hyacinths in the middle and the hyacinths in the background. Do not keep the bowl in a warm place. Bring the plants inside or cover them if the temperature drops to freezing.

A bowl of yellow narcissi

Narcissi are fresh and cheerful – use several shades of one colour or one colour only.
Plants for a bowl with a diameter of 30 cm (12 in):
4 pots of cyclamen narcissi, *Narcissus cyclamineus* "Tête à Tête" (4-5 bulbs per pot)
Planting and care: Water the narcissi bulbs only sparingly after planting them and stand the bowl in a semi-shady position so that the narcissi will flower longer. Fertilize after one week, plant them out in the garden when the flowers are over and fertilize again. Do not remove the foliage until it has turned yellow.

My tip: Small wild narcissi or small-flowered rockery narcissi look particularly attractive in a container.

Warning: Narcissus bulbs are toxic.

A spring box for a sunny position.

A colourful spring box

This will provide flowers right through to early summer.
Plants for a 60-cm (24 in) box:
3 wallflower plants, *Cheiranthus cheiri*
2 daisies, *Bellis perennis*
3 forget-me-nots, *Myosotis* hybrids
2 tulips, *Tulipa* hybrids
Planting and care: Buy the flowering plants in the spring and arrange them in a box with the wallflowers to one side and in the centre background. Place one tall tulip beside them, in the background as well as in the centre of the box. Plant the forget-me-nots and daisies in groups to the right and left, so that one of each is leaning foward slightly over the edge of the box. Stand the group in a sunny to semi-shady position. Water regularly and fertilize once a week. Remove all deadheads.
Wallflowers, daisies and forget-me-nots can be removed after they have finished flowering and can be replaced with summer flowers like pelargoniums, petunias, heliotrope, marguerites or verbena.

An Easter bowl in shades of violet.

Narcissi.

Ideas for the spring

Winter jasmine often flowers in mid-winter.

Try some of these enchanting arrangements which flower from early spring right through to early summer.

and, between them, alternate pachysandra and ivy. Keep everything well moistened and fertilize thoroughly once a week during the summer months. This arrangement can be overwintered outside with some protection and watered on frost-free days.

A box for children

This box provides cheerful little flower faces and delicious treats.
Plants for a 60-cm (24 in) box:
12 pansies, *Viola wittrockiana* hybrids, "Rokoko" mixture
6 alpine strawberry plants, *Fragaria vesca*
Planting and care:
Choose a frost-proof container! Buy the plants in the first month of autumn, mix them when planting and water well. Stand the box in a sunny, bright position and cover it with brushwood for protection as soon as the frosts begin. Keep it moist even in winter. From the first month of spring onwards, remove the brushwood protection as the pansies will already be forming buds. Fertilize well every fortnight from the last month of spring. With proper care you should be able to enjoy the small strawberries right through until the autumn. If the strawberry plants grow too much, cut a few leaves off with scissors. They will grow back again.

First flowers – all in yellow

This is a natural-looking, evergreen, permanent arrangement for semi-shady positions.
Plants for a 60-cm (24 in) box:
1 winter jasmine, *Jasminum nudiflorum*
3 pachysandra, *Pachysandra terminalis*
3 ivies, *Hedera helix* "Arborescens"
1 pot of daffodils, *Narcissus pseudonarcissus*
Planting and care:
Choose a frost-proof container! Place the narcissi in the background to one side, then the jasmine at the front on the other side

A charming box of pansies and alpine strawberries.

A whole range of spring flowers.

A colourful spring bowl

The best loved spring flowers are placed together in this arrangement.
Plants for a bowl with a diameter of 30 cm (12 in):
2 pots of red tulips
(3 bulbs per pot), *Tulipa praestans* "Füsilier"
1 pot blue hyacinths
(3 bulbs per pot),
Hyacinthus orientalis "Bismarck"
2 pots of grape hyacinths
(5 bulbs per pot), *Muscari aucheri*
1 pot of yellow crocuses
(3-5 bulbs per pot),
Crocus chrysanthus
2 pots of snowdrops
(3-5 bulbs per pot),
Galanthus nivalis
Planting and care: Buy the flowering plants in the spring and plant them immediately. Stand them in a frost-free, semi-shady position inside or on a balcony. The bowl can be replanted with other plants after the flowers are over.

My tip: You can obtain the bulbs in the autumn and plant them close together at a depth which is double their height. The frost-proof bowl should be placed in a sheltered position on a balcony, covered with brushwood, straw or wood shavings and watered on frost-free days. As soon as the first shoot tips appear, remove the covering. The arrangement can remain outside all spring if it has been overwintered in this way.

A blue box of tulips

Plants for a 60-cm (24 in) box (painted blue or as you please):
6 different-coloured wallflower plants, *Cheiranthus cheiri*
5 tulip bulbs, *Tulipa* "Queen of Night"
1 tulip bulb, *Tulipa* "Black Parrot"
Planting and care:
Choose a frost-proof container!

Plant the wallflowers and tulip bulbs in the first month of autumn, placing the bulbs about 5 cm (2 in) deep and in two groups in the background. Overwinter the box outside with some protection. Water sparingly on frost-free days. After the bulbs start producing shoots in the spring, stand the box in a spot sheltered from the wind and fertilize once a week.

Dark tulips and colourful wallflowers.

Summer ideas

For the balcony gardener, the summer begins after those final, often rather chilly, days of the last month of spring. Now, at last, you can begin putting frost-sensitive balcony plants outside.

You will find the largest selection of balcony plants for the summer in markets, garden centres and nurseries from around the middle of the second month of spring. You should proceed to order seeds or seedlings of rarer, specialist balcony plants as soon as you receive the latest catalogues or plant lists from the nurseries and seed merchants. Often, only a limited stock is available and this is soon sold out. If you delay ordering until the main season has started, you may find that the mail order firm is overworked and you will receive your seeds and plants much too late.

Creating successful displays

Depending on what plants you choose and how you place them, green oases can be conjured out of grey concrete deserts, open balconies transformed into intimate, cosy nooks and small gardens coaxed into yielding a harvest of berries and vegetables.

A standard plant as an eyecatching centrepiece: Balcony and large container plants trained into a standard form are a decorative and romantic ornament for any balcony. If trimmed into a spherical shape on a long stem or formed into an open, flowering pyramid, heliotrope, daisies, pelargoniums, *Lantana camara*, bay and many other plants can be enjoyed from different angles and perspectives and on more than one level. With standard plants, try adding a delicate-looking underplanting which hangs down over the edge of the container, e.g. sweet alyssum (*Alyssum maritimum*), lobelia (*Lobelia erinus*), Swan River daisies (*Brachycome iberidifolia*) or verbena (*Verbena* hybrids), which can all be overwintered. The advantage is that an arrangement incorporating a standard plant gives you the means of decorating a fairly large area of a corner of a small balcony with flowers.

Espaliers, shelves or flower "steps": Think of a clever way of arranging the plant containers on your balcony early on so that you can accommodate as many plants as possible in a limited space. You will find many aids for this in the gardening trade:

● espaliers and trellises for the wall to help plants to climb;
● space-saving wall shelves made of different materials;
● flower "steps" will allow you to create a decorative arrangement of boxes and pots;
● flowerpot holders for hanging on espaliers or balcony railings (see illustration 7, p. 15);
● hanging containers, using the ceiling or projecting balcony roof (see illustration 1, p. 14).

Visual screens supporting climbing plants: If you are the owner of a proper balcony railing with bars, you could allow plants to climb up and along this by standing containers holding climbing plants at the foot of the railing. Morning glory, black-eyed Susan, *Campanula*, sweet peas and nasturtiums are rapid climbers which will provide privacy from neighbours within one summer. Such greenery will also keep out dust from the road and create a favourable mini-climate.

Berries, herbs and vegetables: A small "allotment" can be created on any balcony that receives plenty of sun. One balcony box alone can provide space for up to six different herbs. Strawberries can even be grown in boxes or hanging containers and black, red and white currants will fruit well if grown as standards in containers with a diameter of 30 cm (12 in). Lettuces, cherry tomatoes, radishes and many salad vegetables will be quite happy with a balcony box as a home. After the last cold snap of spring, leave some runner bean seeds to soak in tepid water overnight and plant them out next day. Runner beans create an attractive and inexpensive profusion of greenery and have pretty red flowers as well as providing food.

A balcony in elegant white with tuber roses, roses, pelargoniums and daisies (from left to right).

A red and yellow summer box

(photo, pp. 16/17)

This can be packed with colourful summer flowers, including pelargoniums, not massed for a change but used to provide bright spots of colour.

Plants for a 60-cm (24 in) box:

2 rudbeckia, *Rudbeckia hirta*
2 marigolds, *Calendula officinalis*
1 red standard pelargonium, *Pelargonium zonale* hybrid "Bundeskanzler"
2 dark blue petunias, *Petunia* hybrids
2 convolvulus, *Convolvulus sabatius*

Planting and care: Buy the flowers in the last month of spring and arrange them in a box with the hanging plants (convolvulus, petunias) in the centre and at the front, leaning slightly forward. The pelargonium is planted in the centre as a colourful marker, and the taller-growing rudbeckia and the marigolds are mixed in the background and along the edges of the box. Take the box outside after the last cold snap of spring and stand it in a sunny to semi-shady spot. Water daily and fertilize thoroughly after three weeks.

Tips on fertilizing

Balcony plants need plenty of nutrients to develop splendid flowers quickly. In this book you will be given advice on fertilizing (if necessary) with the planting plan. In any case, you should never commence fertilizing until three to four weeks after planting as bought plants are usually pre-fertilized.

Ideas for the summer

Try different ways of using perlargoniums. These ever-popular plants are a favourite among balcony gardeners because they are full of colour, flower profusely and are robust and versatile in arrangements. They come as uprights, semi-hanging as well as hanging and even as standards.

Pelargoniums with nasturtiums

This suggests a country garden filled with plants which grow luxuriantly.
Plants for a 60-cm (24 in) box:
1 purple red, upright pelargonium, *Pelargonium zonale* hybrid "Kardinal"
2 pink hanging pelargoniums, cascade varieties
2 pots of low-growing nasturtiums (or seeds), *Tropaeolum* hybrids

Planting and care: The purple red "Kardinal" should be placed at the back on the left, the hanging pelargoniums in the centre at the front and diagonally across the right-hand edge of the container. The cascade varieties will rapidly form very long shoots. Plant the nasturtiums between the pelargoniums and, after they have started shooting, thin them out to just two seedlings each. Stand in full sunshine but protected from rain. Water plentifully every day and, after four weeks, fertilize weekly. The pelargoniums can be overwintered in a frost-free position and then planted together with annuals the following year.

Pelargonium standards

This is an investment that will last for many years with a changeable underplanting.
Plants for a large container with a diameter of 35 cm (14 in):
1 pelargonium standard, *Pelargonium* hybrid

4 *Calocephalus brownii*
Planting and care: Place the standard in the large container, surround it with underplanting, then position it in a sunny spot that should be sheltered from the rain. Water well. Thereafter, water daily and fertilize weekly. Take it inside before the first frosts.

Pelargoniums and nasturtiums.

A standard pelargonium with an underplanting.

Red and white hanging pelargoniums.

Pelargoniums with blue cornflowers

This arrangement is for a sunny spot that is sheltered from the wind.
Plants for a 60-cm (24 in) box:
2 red, upright pelargoniums, *Pelargonium zonale* hybrids
2 red, upright pelargoniums with white-edged leaves, *Pelargonium zonale* hybrids
2 low-growing chrysanthemums, *Chrysanthemum frutescens*
2 cornflowers, *Centaurea cyanus*
Planting and care: Buy the flowers in the last month of spring and plant both the pelargoniums and chrysanthemums alternately in the box. The ones at the front should lean slightly over the edge of the box. Plant the cornflowers in the background. If they are still small, the pelargoniums and chrysanthemums will have to be trimmed back occasionally so that they do not swamp the cornflowers. For this reason, try to buy very robust specimens of cornflowers. Stand the box in a sunny to semi-shady position in a spot sheltered from the wind, water the plants well and fertilize after four weeks. Take them inside before the first frosts and remove the cornflowers.

My tip: Regularly cut off the deadheads. This will stimulate the plants to produce more flowers.

A hanging container with red and white pelargoniums

This arrangement will guarantee continuous flowering all summer and should last for many years.
Plants for a hanging container with a diameter of 30 cm (12 in)
1 white hanging pelargonium, *Pelargonium peltatum* hybrid
2 hanging pelargoniums, 1 red, 1 white and red variety (e.g. "Mexikanerin" or "Rio"), *Pelargonium peltatum* hybrids
Planting and care: Plant the pelargoniums loosely distributed in the container and water well. Planting them close together is not recommended as they will be unable to develop properly during the summer. In regions with a harsher climate, do not put the plants outside until after the last cold snap at the end of spring. Water plentifully daily, remove dead flowers and leaves and fertilize weekly. On very hot days, immerse the entire container in a bath of water once a week. Allow it to drain off well afterwards as pelargoniums do not like waterlogging. Shorten the longest shoots before the first frosts and take the container indoors.

My tip: Do not choose the very popular balcony favourites, cascade hybrids, for your hanging containers. They form extremely long shoots (up to 1.2 m/48 in) and have a very even distribution of foliage and flowers. For hanging containers it is preferable to choose varieties with flower umbels that can be clearly distinguished.

Pelargoniums with cornflowers and daisies.

Ideas for the summer

Old favourites in new settings: popular old-fashioned balcony plants with masses of flowers will give a hint of nostalgia.

A shady box of begonias

Tuber begonias and busy lizzies guarantee a profusion of flowers, even in a semi-shady to shady position.

Plants for a 60-cm (24 in) box:
4 tuber begonias (2 red, 1 orange, 1 yellow), *Begonia* hybrids (tubers) 3 busy lizzies, *Impatiens walleriana* (this is the white/red variety "Belizzy Rotstern")

Planting and care: Buy the plants in the middle of the last month of spring. The two-coloured busy lizzies will open up the rather heavy-looking mass of large-flowered begonias a little. The yellow tuber begonia should be placed in the centre of the box and allowed to lean slightly diagonally across the edge of the box. The other flowers should be grouped around it. Place the box in a semi-shady or shady spot that is sheltered from wind and water well. Always water plentifully, but avoid waterlogging. Three weeks after planting, start fertilizing once a week. If the begonia tubers are large enough, they can be overwintered. After the first frost, cut off the plant 3 cm (1 in) above the tuber. Carefully remove the tuber from the compost and store it in an airy, dry place at 5-10° C (41-50° F) until it starts to shoot in late winter/early spring. Then plant it in moist compost and allow it to shoot in a bright, warm position. Do not overwinter busy lizzies.

Black-eyed Susan

A lovely arrangement can be created with these little golden flower faces.

Plants for a large container with a diameter of 35 cm (14 in):
4 black-eyed Susan, *Thunbergia alata*

Planting and care: Before planting (from the end of spring onwards) push two or three bamboo sticks into the compost in the shape of a wigwam and tie them together at the top. Insert the plants and train three of them upwards and one to climb around the large container. Stand them in a sunny position, sheltered from the wind, water the plants well and fertilize them weekly.

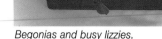

Begonias and busy lizzies.

Black-eyed Susan.

Petunias and busy lizzies.

Pretty in pink

This arrangement uses tireless, continuous-flowering plants which will also flower profusely in semi-shade. They are also thirsty plants whose flowers are, nevertheless, sensitive to rain.

Plants for a 60-cm (24 in) box:
3 busy lizzies in shades of pink, *Impatiens* New Guinea hybrids
2 violet petunias, *Petunia* hybrids
2 scented pelargoniums (here, species with a pine fragrance), *Pelargonium fragrans*

Planting and care: Plant the scented pelargoniums at both ends of the box, leaning slightly over the edge. Plant the petunias and one busy lizzy in the background and place the other two *Impatiens* hybrids in the foreground. Stand the box in a semi-shady position that is sheltered from the rain and water well. Water plentifully daily and start fertilizing weekly after three weeks. Regularly pick out the dead flowers and leaves of the petunias.

My tip: Be sure to take this box inside in good time before the first autumn frosts and remove the petunias. Scented pelargoniums and busy lizzies make beautiful indoor plants during the winter if kept in a cool, bright window.

Warning: Petunias are members of the toxic nightshade family of plants.

Lantana camara

To create an arrangement that is both enchanting and rustic, plant Swan River daisy *(Brachycome iberidifolia)* and *Lantana camara* side by side. Their complementary colours combine to make each other glow.

Plants for a 60-cm (24 in) box:
1 Swan River daisy, *Brachycome iberidifolia*
1 yellow lantana, *Lantana camara* hybrid
1 pansy, *Viola cornuta*
1 small borage plant (or seeds), *Borago officinalis*

Planting and care: The pansy should be planted at one end of the box, the Swan River daisy at the other. Between them, plant the *Lantana camara* leaning slightly across the front edge of the box. Place the borage behind it. Stand the box in a very sunny position and water well. Water sparingly and, three weeks after planting, begin to fertilize every two weeks.

Cut back any lanky shoots of the lantana according to your own judgement. Regularly remove the deadheads of the daisies. Borage, which is an annual, cannot be overwintered. Daisies, lantana and pansies can be kept through the winter in a bright, almost dry position at a temperature of 6-10° C (43-50° F).

Warning: All parts of the lantana are toxic.

Swan River daisies and Lantana camara.

Ideas for the summer

Colourful flowers all summer long.

A composition in shades of gold

If you wish an arrangement that will flower from midsummer to mid-autumn, try using romantic garden flowers such as *Crocosmia* and *Tagetes*.
Plants for a 60-cm (24 in) box:
20 crocosmia bulbs, *Crocosmia* hybrids
3 small-flowered, single, brownish-orange tagetes, *Tagetes tenuifolia*
3 double, low-growing, yellow *Tagetes patula*
Planting and care: Buy the bulbs at the beginning of the last month of spring. Plant them at a depth of about 8 cm (about 3 in) in the background, then alternate dark- and light-coloured flowering tagetes in front. The box should be placed in a sunny position, sheltered from the wind (the crocosmia can grow up to 60 cm/24 in tall), water regularly and fertilize weekly. The tagetes are annuals but crocosmias can be taken out, just like gladioli, and bedded in dry peat for the winter.

My tip: When putting together arrangments using varying shades of the same colour, make sure that the container also matches the colours.

Convolvulus, Cape asters and colourful Nemesia.

A hanging container with delicate flowers

This is an arrangement that will provide flowers in glowing colours all summer long.
Plants for a hanging container with a diameter of 30 cm (12 in)
1 convolvulus, *Convolvulus sabatius*
3 nemesia, *Nemesia* hybrids
1 *Felicia amelloides*
Planting and care: Place the bushy-growing *Felicia* in the background and the *Convolvulus* and the *Nemesia* in the foreground slanting diagonally across the edge of the box. Water well and hang up in a bright position. Fertilize weekly. Cutting back deadheads and shoots throughout the summer will encourage branching and the formation of more flowers. Overwintering is possible for all except the *Nemesia*.

Harmony in shades of gold – Tagetes and Crocosmia.

A box of fuchsias in shades of red

Fuchsias flower profusely all year round, particularly in a semi-shady position.

Plants for a 60-cm (24 in) box:
3 upright fuchsias, *Fuchsia* hybrids
3 semi-hanging or hanging fuchsias, *Fuchsia* hybrids

Planting and care: Place the upright varieties in the background and the semi-hanging and hanging varieties diagonally across the front edge of the box. Water well, stand in a shady to semi-shady position and fertilize weekly. Regularly remove any dead parts.
Take the box indoors before the first frosts and store it in a frost-free place.

My tip: Fuchsias can be bought in several shades of red but the only colour that will go with them is white. When buying fuchsias, make sure that you choose pastel-coloured ones to go with darker-coloured, double and single varieties. This will create a box full of contrasts.

An elegant box in shades of yellow and violet

This arrangement produces an attractive, colourful display in a classical structure with a delicate scent of vanilla and masses of flowers. This summer box will last for one year in a sunny position.

Plants for a 60-cm (24 in) box:
1 sage plant, *Salvia farinacea*
2 heliotrope plants, *Heliotropium arborescens*
3 calceolaria, *Calceolaria integrifolia*

Planting and care: Buy the plants in the last month of spring. Plant the calceolaria close to the edge of the box, leaning towards the front and hanging over the edge, the heliotrope plants in the centre and towards the back, and the tallest plant, the sage, right at the back. Stand the box in a sunny position that is sheltered from the rain.

Water daily and fertilize weekly after three weeks. We do not recommend overwintering the box: calceolaria is an annual and would have to be cut right down for overwintering. Heliotrope is a perennial, but tends not to grow so densely during its second year and is difficult to overwinter (bright at 12-15° C/54-59° F). The sage mentioned here is generally only grown for one year as it is not hardy.

Warning: Heliotrope plants are toxic.

Fuchsias all in shades of red and pink.

Heliotrope and calceolaria.

Ideas for the summer

Fascinating and fragrant rarities for collectors.

A box of herbs

This grouping produces a delicate scent and fresh herbs for the kitchen.

Plants for a 60-cm (24 in) box:
2 Sanvitalia procumbens
1 cotton lavender, Santolina chamae-cyparissus
1 rosemary plant, Rosmarinus officinalis
1 variegated sage, Salvia officinalis "Tricolor"
1 lavender, Lavandula angustifolia
1 fleabane, Erigeron karvinskianus
2-4 sunflower seeds, Helianthus annuus

Planting and care: Place the Sanvitalia plants to the left and right, the lavender and rosemary at the back. The cotton lavender, sage and flea-bane should be planted at the front. Push the sunflower seeds into the compost between the other plants. Water and stand the box in a very sunny position, sheltered from the wind, and fertilize every two weeks. The box can be placed in a bright, cool position or outside if given some protection. The Sanvitalia, sunflowers and fleabane are annuals and will have to be replaced the following year.

A citrus tree with lavender

Create a Mediterranean atmosphere on a very sunny balcony.

Plants for a large container with a diameter of 50 cm (20 in):
1 orange tree, x Citrofortunella mitis
2 lavender plants, Lavandula angustifolia

Planting and care: Use standard potting compost mixed with quartz sand. Plant the standard and the lavender together. Use only soft water for watering and fertilize weekly. Cut back the lavender a little before the first frosts and overwinter the container in a bright, almost dry position at 12-16° C (54-61° F).

Fragrant herbs and a mass of tiny flowers.

Orange tree with blue lavender.

White Polianthes tuberosa, Reseda odorata and other scented plants.

A box of tuber roses

The fragrance of tuber roses, heliotrope and *Reseda* is particularly strong in the evening.

Plants for a 60-cm (24 in) box:
1 lavender, *Lavandula angustifolia*
1 basil plant, *Ocimum basilicum*
2 scented reseda plants, *Reseda odorata*
1 heliotrope, *Heliotropium arborescens*
1 scented pelargonium, *Pelargonium fragrans*
3 tuber roses, *Polianthes tuberosa*

Planting and care: Start off the tubers in the first month of spring. Cover them with compost in a pot standing in a frost-free, bright and dry position. Do not water until the first shoot tips begin to appear. Plant all the plants from the middle of the last month of spring onwards. Place the tuber roses, reseda and heliotrope on one side, and the lavender and basil on the other, with the scented pelargoniums in between. Stand the box in a sunny position, water well and fertilize weekly after four weeks. Scented pelargoniums and heliotrope can be over-wintered indoors in a warm place; lavender can be overwintered outside with some form of protection. The other plants will only live for one year in the box.

Warning: Heliotrope is toxic.

A box of colourful tobacco plants

Plants for a 60-cm (24 in) box:
1 pink ornamental tobacco plant, *Nicotiana x sanderae*
1 red ornamental tobacco plant, *Nicotiana alata*
1 tobacco plant with light green bellflowers, *Nicotiana langsdorffii*
1 white nierembergia, *Nierembergia hippomanica*
5 coloured *Salpiglossis sinuata*
1 *Solanum tuberosum*

Planting and care: Out of all these fairly rare summer plants, only the ornamental tobacco is available as a young plant. The others will have to be grown from seed during the second month of spring. Do not plant them out until the middle of the last month of spring. Place the yellow green bellflower tobacco plant on one side in the background and use the *Solanum* as a counterweight on the other side, about 5 cm (2 in) deep. The *Nierembergia* should be planted in the foreground, leaning at an angle over the edge of the box, and all the other tobacco plant varieties distributed between them. Stand the box in a sunny to semi-shady position, sheltered from the wind, water well and keep it evenly moist. Fertilize thoroughly after two weeks. The annuals cannot be overwintered.

Warning: All parts of these plants are toxic.

A beautiful display of tobacco plants.

Ideas for the autumn

The warm, mild days of autumn are blessed with bright red fruits and glowing, golden orange leaves. Try to think ahead when you make your purchases in the spring and choose plants with interesting autumn foliage that also bear decorative, brilliant red berries.

A quick way to autumn splendour

Most nurseries and garden centres offer a wide range of possibilities for decorating balconies with flowers and berries. Most of these plants are available from the end of summer onwards, can cope with temperatures just around freezing and will flower until late autumn:
● hebe in shades of white, wine red and violet, *Hebe x andersonii* hybrids
● chrysanthemums in shades of white, yellow, gold, bronze, rose and violet, *Chrysanthemum indicum* hybrids
● China asters in shades of white, rose, violet and blue, *Callistephus chinensis*

● winter-flowering heather in white and red, *Erica gracilis*
● heather in shades of white and rose violet, *Erica herbacea*
● autumn asters from various species, as well as different shades of white, rose, red, and blue, *Aster dumosus, Aster amellus, Aster novae-angliae*
● senecio with silvery leaves, *Senecio bicolor*
● calocephalus, with a fine web of delicate twigs, *Calocephalus brownii*

Attractive fruits and colourful leaves

A number of hardy woody plants are very suitable for growing in large contain-ers or troughs. If you are keen on having a balcony full of autumn colour, you should choose species and varieties that display attractive, colourful foliage in the autumn or bear bright berries. The best way to help these plants through the winter is if you buy and plant them as early as springtime. This will give them a chance to develop a healthy root system during the summer and they will bear berries and bright foliage in the autumn of the same year. Always pick frost-proof, roomy containers for these plants as the plants will last for many years and – with an underplanting of seasonal flowers – will make a beautiful picture all year round.

Shrubs with decorative fruits
● rose, *Rosa rugosa* "Frau Dagmar Hastrup" has single pink flowers and large red hips in the autumn
● firethorn, *Pyracantha coccinea* "Orange Charmer"; clusters of white flowers with bunches of orange berries in the autumn
● *Cotoneaster*; all species of this genus bear red berries in the autumn. Cotoneaster species grow between 20-300 cm (8-120 in) tall.

My tip: Many nurseries now offer *Pernettya mucronata* during the autumn for a quick plant-ing and display. However, this attractive, evergreen shrub with bunches of red berries is not frost-resistant and needs some protection in the winter.

Shrubs with attractive autumn colouring
● snowy mespilus, *Amelanchier lamarckii*; orange-red autumn colouring, edible fruits
● sumach, *Rhus typhina*; glowing orange autumn colouring, candle-shaped fruits in shades of purple to rose pink

Autumn preparations

Collect the seeds of summer annuals. These can be put in paper bags and stored in a warm, dry, dark place. Bulbous plants that flower in the spring should be bought and planted now (see p. 22). Autumn is also the right time to plant biennial spring flowering plants like forget-me-not, wallflowers and pansies. Plant the young plants out during the autumn and overwinter them with some form of protection

Red gold autumn colours
Bathed in soft autumn sunlight – Erica, autumn crocus (left), hebe and myrtle (in the bowl), grasses and a clipped box tree (right).

Ideas for the autumn

Try these suggestions for quick arrangements of enchanting autumn plants.

A box of asters in shades of pink

Mix various shades of pink and violet, using large and small flowers together.
Plants for a 60-cm (24 in) box:
6 pink and violet China asters, *Callistephus chinensis*
4 pink cushion asters, *Aster dumosus* hybrids
Planting and care: These plants can be bought from the end of summer. Alternate large- and small-flowering varieties in the box, allowing the plants at the front to incline slightly over the edge of the box. Make sure that the silhouette of the planting presents a closed, even aspect. The flowers will cope with both sunlight and shade. Water well and always keep the compost moist. The large-flowered China asters are annuals and cannot be overwintered but the smaller-flowering cushion asters are perennials and can be planted out in the garden.

Coreopsis and coneflower

If yellow is your favourite colour, here is a planting of hardy perennials that will last for many years.
Plants for a large container with a diameter of 50 cm (20 in):
1 coneflower, *Rudbeckia fulgida* var. *sullivantii* "Goldsturm"
1 coreopsis, *Coreopsis grandiflora* "Early Sunrise"
1 anthemis, *Anthemis tinctoria* "Grallagh Gold"
1 spurge, *Euphorbia coralloides*

Planting and care: Make sure to choose a frost-proof container, as this will enable the plants to overwinter outside for years. Buy the plants as solitary, flowering plants in the summer. Set the coneflower and the coreopsis as a group in the background, and plant the anthemis and spurge in front, leaning forward over the edge of the container. Stand the container in a sunny position, sheltered from the wind, water well and fertilize once after three weeks. Do not cut off the attractive seedheads. During the winter, they will look enchanting when covered in a dusting of frost.

A box of pink asters.

A yellow arrangement for the golden days of autumn.

Yellow chrysanthemums and Cotoneaster with berries.

An autumn bowl with berries

A quick planting with possibilites for variations.
Plants for a bowl with a diameter of 60 cm (24 in):
1 cotoneaster with red berries, *Cotoneaster horizontalis*
3 yellow chrysanthemums, *Chrysanthemum indicum* hybrids
2 senecio, *Senecio bicolor*
1 *Calocephalus brownii*
Planting and care: These plants should be available from early autumn onwards. The *Cotoneaster* should be set in the centre so that it is able to unfold its decorative branches freely. Plant the chrysanthemums in a bunch together to make a colourful centre point. The silver grey of the *Senecio* and the *Calocephalus* will seem to draw them together. The bowl will cope with all conditions of light and must be kept evenly moist. After the annual chrysanthemum has finished flowering, the *Cotoneaster* can be planted out in the garden.
Alternatives: Substitute branches of rosehips or holly with berries for the *Cotoneaster* and replace the faded chrysanthemums with *Erica*.

A colourful autumn box

The photograph below shows what a box looks like when it has not been cleared out completely after each season. The pansies have flowered right through spring and summer, and the marigolds and *Calocephalus* come from a summer planting.
Plants for a 60-cm (24 in) box:
3 perennial asters in various shades of pink, *Aster dumosus*
3 chrysanthemums (2 salmon pink, 1 yellow), *Chrysanthemum indicum* hybrids
2 senecios, *Senecio bicolor*
1 *Calocephalus brownii*
1 yellow marigold, *Calendula officinalis*
1 yellow pansy, *Viola wittrockiana* hybrid
Planting and care: If you want to restock this box in the autumn, you will have to make do without the marigold which is a summer plant. Place the tall-growing asters at the back and, in front, to left and right, the chrysanthemums. Plant the grey-leaved senecio hanging slightly over one of the sides of the box and in the centre. Plant the *Calocephalus* and the pansy in the centre foreground. Stand the box in a position that is sheltered from the wind, and water it well. Cover it with newspaper in frosty weather.

An autumn kaleidoscope of asters and chrysanthemums.

Ideas for the autumn

Somewhat surreal – ornamental cabbages in a box.

These enchanting plantings display all their beauty during the autumn.

Ornamental cabbages in a flower box

This makes a most unusual and eyecatching arrangement.

Plants for a 60-cm -(24 in) box:

4 ornamental cabbage plants, *Brassica oleracea*

Planting and care: These fully grown cabbage plants are offered for sale in early autumn. Buy them in various different colours and sizes. Plant the tallest one a little off-centre and towards the front and group the others (of different heights) at intervals around it. Press the compost down firmly so that the plants cannot tip over and water well. The box can be placed anywhere but cannot be overwintered.

My tip: Decorate the box with foliage, moss and chestnuts.

Autumn crocuses in grass

A very undemanding, perpetual box which is quite lovely in the autumn.

Plants for a 60-cm (24 in) box:

8 festuca plants, *Festuca cinerea*

6 Autumn crocus bulbs, *Colchicum autumnale*

Planting and care:

Choose a frost-proof container for a permanent planting. The best time to plant is late summer as the bulbs of the autumn crocus should be available then. Soil mixed with sand makes an ideal compost for these plants. Plant the *Festuca* plants in a slightly staggered formation and push the bulbs in to a depth of about 4 cm (1½ in) between them. Water well but do not fertilize. The box can be placed in a sunny to semi-shady position and later overwintered outside. Do not cut off the leaves of the autumn crocus which appear in the spring until they have turned brown.

My tip: This box will be a wonderful sight in the spring as well if you plant a few crocuses and/or tulip bulbs in between the grasses in the autumn.

Warning: autumn crocuses are toxic!

Sunflowers in a trough

A permanent planting with annual sunflowers as the main feature.

Plants for a trough

70 cm (28 in) long, 40 cm (16 in) wide, 60 cm (24 in high):

1 *Cotoneaster dielsianus*

5 ivy plants, *Hedera helix*

5 sunflower plants, *Helianthus annuus*

Planting and care:

Choose a frost-proof container as this planting can be overwintered outside. Plant the permanent plants (ivy and *Cotoneaster*) in the spring. Plant the young sunflower plants in the background during late spring/early summer, water plentifully and, after four weeks, begin to fertilize every two weeks. A position that is semi-shady and sheltered from the wind is ideal.

Autumn crocuses among Festuca grass.

The sunflowers will form huge seedheads which are in great demand among birds and still look attractive in the winter. Overwinter the box with a protective covering of brushwood. Remove the sunflower plants during late spring of the following year and plant new ones or choose other seasonal plants.

My tip: Tall dahlias and perennial asters are very suitable for this purpose, or try runner beans which will climb among the branches of the Cotoneaster.

Hebes all in violet

An autumn planting for those who love violet.
Plants for a 60-cm (24 in) box:
5 violet hebes, Hebe andersonii hybrids
1 wine red hebe, Hebe andersonii hybrid
Planting and care: Plant all the plants at staggered intervals in the box. The red hebe should be placed slightly to one side to create a good effect. Place the box in a sheltered position and water it well. If you want to enjoy these plants for many years, you will have to take them inside before the first frosts start. Their winter quarters should be bright and cool (8-10° C/ 46-50° F) and they should not be given much water during this period. In the following spring, they should be repotted in fresh compost and taken outside from the last month of spring. Here, they should receive fertilizer every fortnight. The plants will not cope with waterlogging and should definitely be placed in a spot that is sheltered from the rain.

My tip: Hebe andersonii hybrids are the only hebe species which are suitable for growing in a box. In addition to the violet and wine red varieties, there are also white-flowering ones and some with green and white leaves. A combination of variegated hebe (Hebe andersonii hybrid "Variegata") and climbing tufted vetch (Vicia cracca) is very attractive.

Sunflowers with Cotoneaster and ivy.

A box planted with hebes.

Ideas for the winter

Winter is the time for evergreens and conifers to make their grand entrance and liven up the uniform greys of a wintery town. At this time of year you must not forget the birds who love to visit balconies full of greenery, particularly if there is food there.

Frost-proof containers

Hardy plantings should be established in containers that are completely frost-proof. The great risk in winter is that the compost inside pots and containers will freeze and expand, causing the container to crack. Terracotta containers soak up water like a sponge and react in the same way during very cold weather. You can avoid this problem if you use plant containers made of wood, concrete, natural stone and plastic. If you still do not wish to give up the beauty of ceramic containers, here are a few tips:
● Choose ceramic containers which have been fired at very high temperatures and are glazed.
● Protect the container with an "overcoat" of polystyrene, bubble pack, straw or brushwood.
● Keep the compost only slightly moist during the winter season and avoid wetting it fully. Stand the containers in spots where no rain or snow can penetrate them.

My tip: Start thinking about protection from frost before planting. Large containers with vertical walls can easily be clad with polystyrene sheets on the inside, which insulate the pot from any kinds of temperature fluctuations and can also serve as a buffer when the contents of the container freeze and expand.

Conifers in containers

Conifers are evergreens which feel quite at home in boxes, troughs and large containers. They thrive in semi-shady positions and should never be allowed to dry out, especially when they are young. Water them plentifully, even on frost-free days in winter when the compost is not frozen through. If the conifers are planted in a large container with plenty of compost, they will not be so likely to dry out. This selection of conifers will remain fairly small:
● Hinoki cypress, *Chamaecyparis obtusa* "Nana Gracilis"; dark green, shiny foliage
● Sawara cypress, *Chamaecyparis pisifera* "Filifera Nana"; fresh green, needle-like foliage
● Chinese juniper, *Juniperus chinensis* "Blaw"; grey blue foliage, like scales
● common juniper, *Juniperus communis* "Repanda"; dark green, silver-striped foliage
● creeping juniper, *Juniperus horizontalis* "Glauca"; steel blue foliage with short needles
● Nepal juniper, *Juniperus squamata* "Blue Star"; silvery blue foliage, pointed and prickly
● Norway spruce, *Picea abies* "Acrocona"; dark green foliage, some of which is very sharply pointed
● Norway spruce, *Picea abies* "Echiniformis"; yellow green to grey green foliage
● Norway spruce, *Picea abies* "Little Gem"; fresh green, very fine foliage
● Norway spruce, *Picea abies* "Pumila Glauca"; blue green, very dense foliage
● mountain pine, *Pinus mugo* "Gnom"; dark green, dense foliage
● mountain pine, *Pinus mugo* "Mops"; dark green foliage, slightly prickly

My tip: Conifer plantings look fresher if they are combined with large-leaved evergreen plants like cherry laurel (*Prunus laurocerasus* "Otto Luyken"), box (*Buxus sempervirens*), evergreen creeping cotoneaster (*Cotoneaster salicifolius* "Herbstfeuer") or ivy (*Hedera helix*).

Warning: All of these plants or parts of them are toxic!

Snow and winter sunshine have transformed this balcony into a fairy kingdom. Evergreen conifers, bushes with red berries, frost-proof garden ornaments and a bird-feeding station will bring colour and life close to your window.

Ideas for the winter

This is the season for evergreen and conifer trees. When winter begins to reduce the colours in nature, the many shades of green of dwarf trees and shrubs become increasingly attractive and even the very smallest flowers stand out in contrast. Always choose a frost-proof container for all winter plantings (see p. 44).

Flowers throughout the winter

It is not impossible to have flowering arrangements from winter to spring. Try some of the following plantings.

Plants for a 60-cm (24 in) box:
5 pink heathers, *Erica herbacea*
2 dwarf brooms, *Cytisus decumbens*
2 festuca plants, *Festuca scoparia*
10 crocus bulbs, *Crocus species*

Planting and care: Buy the plants in the autumn as soon as heather is available. Mix the compost with sand. Plant the broom at a slight angle so that the branches droop gently across the edge of the box. Plant the *Festuca* between the *Erica* and set the crocus bulbs in groups between them at a depth of about 4 cm (1½ in). Water well and stand in a sunny to semi-shady position. Also water in winter in frost-free weather. The dwarf broom will produce golden yellow flowers in early spring, shortly after which time the crocuses will also appear.

My tip: Instead of crocus bulbs you could also plant other spring flowers, e.g. snowdrops (*Galanthus nivalis*), winter aconite (*Eranthis hiemalis*) or grape hyacinths (*Muscari aucheri*).

Large containers for all seasons

This permanent planting gives flowers in spring, summer and autumn plus shades of green in winter.

Plants for a container with a diameter of 45 cm (18 in):
1 common juniper, *Juniperus communis*
1 shrubby cinquefoil, *Potentilla fruticosa* "Red Ace"
1 dwarf rohododendron, *Rhododendron repens* hybrid "Scarlet Wonder"
1 dwarf mountain pine, *Pinus mugo* "Pumilio"

Planting and care: The best time for planting is in the first and second months of autumn. Set the juniper in the background. The cinquefoil and the dwarf pine should lean slightly over the edge of the container. Plant the rohododendron with ericaceous compost surrounding the roots. Stand the container in a semishady position and water regularly – even in winter on frost-free days. In the spring, fertilize every four weeks with liquid fertilizer.

Winter heather with broom and crocuses.

Attractive shades of green.

Conifers with a small-flowering cushion plant.

Conifers in a box

A group of evergreens will last for many years. Mix them with small-flowering plants for contrast.
Plants for a 60-cm (24 in) box:
1 creeping juniper, *Juniperus horizontalis* "Glauca"
1 Nepal juniper, *Juniperus squamata* "Loderis"
1 small Sawara cypress, *Chamaecyparis pisifera squarrosa* "Boulevarus"
1 blue Lawson cypress, *Chamaecyparis lawsoniana* "Ellwoodii"
1 evergreen euonymus, *Euonymus fortunei* "Gracilis"
1 pansy, *Viola cornuta* "Princess Blue"
1 bugle, *Ajuga reptans* "Atropurpurea"
1 white arabis, *Arabis procurrens*

Planting and care: Plant during the first and second months of autumn. Plant the cypress species and the Nepal juniper at staggered intervals. The *Euonymus* should be set to one side and the hardy cushion plants (bugle and arabis) and the *Juniperus horizontalis* planted to hang over the front edge of the box. The bugle will bear violet blue flowers in late spring and early summer, the arabis displays white flowers on 10 cm (4 in) tall stalks in late spring. The *Viola cornuta* should be planted towards the centre. Water even in winter on frost-free days! In the spring, dissolve special conifer fertilizer in water and feed the plants.

A Christmas arrangement

Mountain pine branches with small cones and coloured balls on sticks make a festive display.
Plants for a 60-cm (24 in) box:
mountain pine branches, *Pinus mugo*
Arranging and care: Try to buy branches with cones and divide them up into 20-40 cm (8-16 in) long sections. Fill a frost-proof container with soil and push the longer branches in at the back and the shorter ones at the front, packed as densely as possible. When you are ready, you can start to decorate the arrangement, e.g. with small glass balls on sticks or weather-resistant Christmas decorations.

My tip: The branches of other evergreen conifers can also be used and are usuallly available in markets and garden centres at this time of year, e.g.:
● mahonia *(Mahonia aquifolium)* with shiny green, prickly foliage
● box *(Buxus sempervirens)* with small, shiny leaves
● silver fir *(Abies nobilis)* with silver grey needles which do not fall off
● holly *(Ilex aquifolium)* with dark green, shiny leaves and red berries
● mistletoe *(Viscum album)* with longish oval, golden green leaves and white berries

An arrangement of conifer branches.

Plant care all year round

If you wish your plants to produce healthy leaves and beautiful flowers, you must do all that you can to create a healthy environment for them. We tend to expect rare feats of flowering splendour from our balcony plants but they will only produce such delights if they are given optimal care.

Overhanging plants enveloping their box
The scented Plectranthus coleoides will produce green-and-white-leaved shoots up to 1 m (40 in) long. Yellow orange nasturtiums (Tropaeolum hybrids), delicate pink Polygonum capitatum "Afghan" and convolvulus (Convolvulus sabatius) bring colour to the ensemble.

49

A lively box of pink petunias, including the large-flowered, double variety "Fanfare".

The right way to plant containers

Good soil and compost are vital if your balcony plants are to thrive. When you buy plants, look for signs of quality and do not take the cheapest plants. When in doubt, ask the garden centre or nursery for the right kind of compost, e.g. are the plants lime lovers or peat lovers.

The right compost

A whole range of composts is suitable for balcony plants. The following points should be considered when choosing compost:
● it should provide a comfortable "bed" and support for the plants;
● it should provide all the important main nutrients and trace elements required by the plants;
● it should store water and nutrients and release them to the plants as required;
● it should remain air-permeable and friable even when used for permanent planting;
● it should be free of disease, weed seeds and pests.

Standard composts are very suitable for balcony plants and are used by many gardeners. They can be bought in different quantities and contain varying ratios of nutrients. Use a standard compost containing basic fertilizer when planting the first time as this compost contains enough nutrients to suffice for the first few weeks.

Balcony plant compost: This label may be found on bags of compost but such a description could apply to many types of compost and is no guarantee of quality or content.

Moss peat compost: Different types of this compost can be found for sale. Some contain higher levels of fertilizer than others and all contain large amounts of moss peat. Moss peat compost containing a low level of fertilizer is more suitable for growing balcony plants. All types can be used for mixing with garden soil. Moss peat compost is not recommended for use on its own.

Seedling composts are very fine, germ-free and fertilizer-free or only lightly fertilized. They are necessary if growing plants from seed or for planting out young plants but not for ready-grown plants.

Home-made balcony plant compost

Garden soil is nearly always too heavy for growing plants in containers. It soon becomes very dense in pots and boxes and is often full of weed seeds. You will obtain a good, light compost for growing plants in containers if you mix 3 parts garden soil with 3 parts well-rotted, sieved garden compost and 2 parts peat or sand. Alternatively, you can use garden soil and standard compost mixed in a ratio of 1:1.

Tips on planting

Every plant that is potted or repotted should be surrounded by at least 2 cm (¾ in) (10 cm/4 in, in the case of larger plants) of fresh compost. This means that you should choose a plant container that is big enough!

● Carefully remove the plant from its pot.

● If you are repotting an older plant, carefully shake out the rootstock and cut off dried up or decayed roots.

● Make sure that larger containers have a drainage layer to prevent waterlogging. For this purpose, it is recommended that you insert a 5-10 cm (2-4 in) thick layer of clay pot shards, Hortag, washed sand or gravel in the bottom of the container. Spread a piece of interfacing fabric over this layer and then fill the container with compost. The fabric will prevent the compost from becoming mixed up with the drainage layer and thereby hindering drainage.

● Insert your plants, pack plenty of compost around them, press down lightly and water the plants.

Correct watering

Not all plants have the same requirements. The frequency of watering and the volume of water required will depend on the plant in question but also on its position and the current weather conditions.

The ideal type of water

Before use, the water should have been left to stand for a while to allow it to be warmed slightly by the sun. It should not be too hard (not above 21 degrees Clark). You can find out the hardness factor of your water from your local water authority. Hard water can be softened with special softening agents from the gardening trade or by inserting a small fabric bag filled with peat in a bucket of mains water for a few hours. Rainwater that has been collected in pollution-free conditions is still the cheapest and best water for balcony plants.

The basic rules of watering

You will have to *water a lot* during the main growth period (mainly in the summer), on sunny, windy balconies, when it is very hot and if there is a drought. Plants which are planted in very peaty compost, as well as in clay containers, will dry out faster than others and will require more water.

Medium watering is required during the spring and autumn, in shady spots sheltered from the wind and on cool, rainy days.

Plants in plastic containers will lose less water through evaporation than those in clay pots and will, therefore, not dry out so quickly.

Watering in the winter: Every so often it may happen that plants do not survive the winter. As often as not, incorrect watering is responsible for this result. What to look out for is explained on page 53.

My tip: During the summer, never water plants in bright sunlight and do not water the leaves. The drops of water can easily act like magnifying glasses and cause the leaves to burn. During the winter, it is preferable to water plants before noon so that they can dry off before nightfall.

Irrigation systems as plant sitters

Not all of us are lucky enough to have friendly neighbours who are willing to look after balcony plants during our absence. In this case there are other ways of solving the problem. The ideal device for short absences (e.g. a weekend) is a flower box with an inbuilt water-storage unit (available in the gardening trade). Even a lengthy holiday absence of three weeks or longer can be overcome without any help from others by installing a fully automatic long-term watering system, connected directly to the mains water supply. There are several irrigation systems which function in different ways and are more or less expensive. Enquire about different systems at your local garden centre and do a trial run before going away on a long absence.

Successful fertilizing

We tend to expect masses and masses of flowers from our balcony plants. However, with the limited volume of compost at their disposal this is only possible if nutrients are provided regularly and in sufficient quantities. The fertilizer contained in the first planting compost will be used up after three to four weeks, so regular fertilizing will have to begin after that.

The nourishment that plants require

In general, a distinction is made between main nutrients, large quantities of which are necessary for the continued well-being of the plants, and trace elements of which only a small dose is required. These latter substances are also called micronutrients.

The main nutrients, which are necessary for the stable structural growth of the plant, are:
● nitrogen (N), required for the formation of leaves;
● phosphorous (P), for the formation of flowers and fruit;
● potassium (K);
● calcium (Ca);
● magnesium (Mg).

Among the trace elements are iron, copper, manganese, molybdenum, zinc and boron.

Compound fertilizers

The most important plant nutrients and trace elements are contained in compound fertilizers. The quantities of individual nutrients are usually indicated on the packaging in the form of the NPK ratio – i.e. 14:7:14 means that this fertilizer contains 14% nitrogen (N), 7% phosphorous (P) and 14% potassium (K).

In mineral or chemical fertilizers, the nutrients are bound with chemical salts and can be absorbed quickly and directly by the plants.

They are immediately effective. Disadvantage: mineral fertilizers are strong and can easily burn roots, particularly if they are dry. This can lead to an excess of mineral salts, particularly in small pots which hold only a small volume of compost.

In organic compound fertilizers (for example, horn, blood, bonemeal, manure), the nutrients have to be broken down by micro-organisms in the soil before they are accessible to the plants. This process is even slower when growing plants in pots than in garden soil, and actual fertilizing is therefore a delayed process. On the other hand, this type of fertilizing encourages the presence of beneficial soil flora and is therefore particularly recommended for permanent plantings. If you want to fertilize quickly in order to have plenty of flowers, you can help the process along with some liquid fertilizer.

Types of fertilizer

Fertilizers are obtainable in solid and liquid form, for watering, sprinkling or spraying on leaves. Liquid fertilizers for mixing with water are recommended as they are easy to apply and use on a regular basis. Another practical form is controlled-release fertilizer which can be mixed into the compost in the form of granules to release nutrients to the plants over a period of ten to twelve weeks.

The golden rules of fertilizing

● Do not start giving regular doses of fertilizer until three to four weeks after planting in pre-fertilized compost.
● If the compost has been mixed with controlled-release fertilizer, do not start fertilizing until ten weeks after planting.
● The best way to employ liquid fertilizer is to mix it with the water used for watering the plants.

● Never tip fertilized water or fertilizer granules on to the leaves (if you do, immediately wash the leaves clean with clear water).
● Only fertilize plants that have moisture round their roots. Dry compost should be watered first.
● It is better to give low doses more frequently than fertilizing seldom but in large amounts!
● If you intend to overwinter plants, do not fertilize them at all from the last month of summer onwards so that their shoots are able to mature properly before they are taken indoors in the autumn.

Overwintering and propagating

At the beginning of winter, containers and perennial plants have to be protected from frost, waterlogging and damage due to dryness. Give some thought beforehand as to which plants will require winter quarters in your house and which plants will be able to survive the cold season in a protected position outside (see tables, p. 20/21).

Overwintering outside

The following plants can overwinter outside: perennials, bulbs, shrubs and small trees (including roses) and biennial flowering plants. These plants are hardy when planted out in the garden, but are at risk from freezing to death or drying out because of the small volume of compost in their containers.

Winter protection
● Permanent plantings, in large containers which are insulated on the inside against temperature fluctuations by the use of polystyrene sheets, can remain where they are and only need some protective covering of straw or conifer branches.
● Containers that are not insulated are best moved close to the house

wall and protected from cold from below by standing them on wooden battens or polystyrene sheets.

● Move the containers close together and pack straw, dead leaves or wood shavings around them.

● Surround a standard plant, from its pot to its crown, with bushy conifer branches and tie these up with thick string. Alternative: wrap the standard in a straw mat.

Watering in the winter: All plants must have a little moisture around their roots when the frosty period begins. Water them with tepid water on frost-free days during the winter. Plants which are overwintered in a roofed-over area will require more water as they will not receive any rain. Make sure the plants are not standing in water (check all drainage holes before winter).

Overwintering plants indoors

Perennial plants which originate from tropical or subtropical regions will have to be overwintered indoors. Warm, dark positions are unsuitable. The optimal winter quarters are cool (2-10° C/36-50° F), bright, airy and dry and easy to ventilate.

● Before taking the plants inside, cut back the shoots and flower stems to the woody parts.

● Keep all the plants dry rather than too moist. The warmer the overwintering space, the brighter it should be and the more often you will need to water the plants.

● Water in the mornings so that the plants have dried off by evening.

● Check for pests frequently.

● Remove dried up or decayed foliage which is a magnet for disease.

● Ventilate the room on mild days.

● Water more often from the end of the second month of winter and stand the plants in a brighter and warmer position.

● During the first month of spring repot the plants in fresh compost.

Convolvulus (Convolvulus sabatius) should be overwintered in a cool position.

Propagating

Propagating from seed and the cultivation of cuttings are the most common methods of propagating balcony plants. Which method you choose will depend on the species of the plant and a few other factors (see p. 9).

Propagating from seed

If you want masses of flowers on your balcony as soon as the last frosts of spring are over, you will have to start sowing seeds indoors or in a mini-propagator before the end of winter. If you are not in a great hurry and have little space indoors for seed trays etc., I recommend sowing directly into seed bowls or balcony containers outside from the middle of the second month of spring onwards. The sowing times indicated on the seed packets will tell you when to sow outside. Very often the germination time is also given.

What you will need for sowing seeds

● Seeds of the plant you wish to grow. Seeds of summer flowers can be obtained as early as the second month of winter in garden centres, seed shops and nurseries.

● Seeding compost which should be germ-free, retain water and be porous. Seeding compost should contain very little or no fertilizer so that the roots are able to develop properly. If you use medium-heavy garden soil, you should pass it through a sieve first and then mix it with one-third standard compost to make it lighter and more porous.

● Seeding trays with a transparent cover, obtainable in the gardening trade. If there are only a few seeds, you can even use an old yoghurt pot with a piece of transparent cling film or a piece of glass as a cover. No matter which type of container you decide to use, it is extremely important to have adequate drainage holes at the bottom.

Method

● Fill the tray evenly with compost (up to 1 cm/½ in below the edge) and moisten it.

● Sow the seeds by scattering them as far apart as possible (see illustration 1). The larger the spaces between the individual seeds, the less time will be spent on thinning out the seedlings after germination.

● Medium-fine and fine seeds should be pressed down lightly by hand or with a flat piece of wood and, using a fine spray on the watering can, watered lightly. Larger seeds should be covered with a thin layer of compost so that they cannot dry out during germination.

● Place the cover on the seedtray (see illustration 2) so that a moist, warm climate is created, and stand the tray in a warm place at about 20° C (68° F). No light is necessary until the first tiny leaves appear.

● Remove the cover from time to time for ventilation.

● As soon as the first tiny leaves appear, remove the cover, stand the tray in as bright a position as possible (at about 12° C/54° F) but protected from direct sunlight.

Pricking out the young plants

As soon as the seedlings appear to be crowding each other, you will have to thin them out. You will need a pricking out tool, pricking out compost (containing small amounts of fertilizer) and small seedling pots. Multi-pot trays (see illustration 5) are very useful as the young plants can be accommodated in very little

1 Scatter the seeds as far apart as possible.

2 The cover will keep the compost moist.

3 As soon as the seedlings start to touch each other, carefully prick them out.

space and still form healthy root-stocks.

Method

● Lift the plants out of the tray with the thin end of the pricking out tool and carefully separate them if they are very close together.

● Shorten the roots (see illustration 4), as this will promote further growth.

● Prepare a small hole in the new container with the blunt end of the pricking out tool and plant the seedling (see illustration 5).

● Press the compost down slightly all around and water thoroughly with the fine-spray attachment of your watering can.

● Stand the pricked out plants in a very bright position at about 12° C (54° F) but protect them from direct sunlight.

Propagation from cuttings

You will be able to take cuttings from perennial plants like pelargoniums or fuchsias during late summer or spring. The parent plant should be robust and healthy at the time of cutting, free of pests and not faded. A good cutting should have one to two fully developed pairs of leaves. Use mature shoots, not very young

6 Take a cutting 1 cm (about ½ in) below the second pair of leaves and plant it in a pot.

7 Pull a plastic bag over crossed wires and tie it up.

ones as they will decay too easily; woody cuttings, on the other hand, will not root well.

What you will need for propagating

● a sharp, clean knife;
● containers with transparent covers; peat pots or peat pellets are very good as the roots will grow right through their walls. The young plants can be planted together with these pots in their final positions;
● seedling compost as used for sowing (see p. 54).

Method

● Remove a cutting about 1 cm (½ in) below the leaf axil of the second pair of leaves of the parent plant (see illustration 6).

● Break off buds and flowers so that the plant will not waste any energy on them.

● Push the cutting into the compost to just above the leaf axil, gently press down the compost and water carefully.

● Place a transparent cover over the cutting (crossed-over wire loops will prevent the cover from touching the leaves and causing decay, see illustration 7).

● Stand the cutting in a bright position at 20ºC (68ºF) but protect it from direct sunlight.

● Keep it moist and air it daily. It may take several weeks before roots have formed. Then remove the cover.

4 Slightly shorten the root tips.

5 Make a hole, insert the seedling and press down lightly.

A water box full of marsh plants.

Pests and diseases

Plants which are not given proper care are more susceptible to pests and diseases than flowers placed in an optimal position and given the correct nutrients. In addition to proper care, there are a number of other ways to prevent infestation.

Preventive measures

● Regularly check your plants and remove sick, dried up or faded parts of plants as well as weeds.
● Clean out used plant containers with a hot soapy solution and then rinse them well in clear water.
● Give your balcony plants some attractive neighbours who will help to keep away pests, e.g. lavender (*Lavandula angustifolia*) to keep away aphids. *Tagetes* species are good against eel worms or nematodes. Nicandra (*Nicandra physalodes*) will keep away aphids.

● Plant tissues can be fortified by spraying the plants with special fortifying agents that are obtainable in the gardening trade.

Mistakes in care

Many of the symptoms of illness we see in plants are simply the result of mistakes in care. Once matters are put right and the plants receive what they require for proper growth and well-being, they will recover and soon form new, healthy shoots and beautiful flowers.

Plants which do not seem to want to flower are usually receiving too much nitrogen and not enough phosphorous/potassium in their fertilizer. A position which is too moist or does not receive enough sunlight can also be responsible for this problem.
Remedy: check the type of fertilizer and dosage and, if necessary, move the plant to another position.
Long, lanky shoots are formed in positions that do not receive enough light.
Remedy: choose a brighter position.
Yellow leaves may indicate several problems at once, e.g. lack of light or nitrogen, overwatering or an old plant.
Remedy: check the position and the fertilizer; check whether the plant is waterlogged.
Leaves that turn pale while the veins remain green. This indicates chlorosis which is caused by a lack of trace elements such as iron or magnesium.
Remedy: only water with soft water, mix an iron preparation with the water and choose a warmer position for the plant.
Red, grey or silver grey spots on the leaves indicate sunburn which occurs if the plant is taken abruptly out into the sun after overwintering or purchase.
Remedy: as a rule, always accustom the plant very gradually to a sunny position outside. Start by choosing a shady or semi-shady position.

Control of pests and diseases
It is not always necessary to reach for highly toxic chemical products as soon as a plant shows symptoms of infestation with pests or disease. Try some of the biological alternatives first, although, admittedly, you will not always find them to be completely reliable and successful.

Natural controls
● Nettle extract to combat aphids. About 500 g (1 lb) fresh nettles should be steeped in 5 litres (9 pt) of water for 12-24 hours. Then spray the plants with the fresh, undiluted brew.
● Garlic brew for fungal infections and spider mites. Take and crush 1 clove of garlic. Pour 1 litre (1¾ pt) of boiling water over it. Allow it to cool, strain and spray undiluted.
● Wormwood brew to combat biting and sucking insects. Pour 1 litre (1¾ pt) of boiling water over 1 tsp wormwood leaves. Allow to cool, strain and spray undiluted.
● Soap solutions penetrate the bodies of insects and prevent them from breathing. The pests rapidly die off.
● Paraffin and white oil are purified, natural oil products which clog the respiratory systems of pests.
● Pyrethrum extract is derived from the flowers of *Chrysanthemum cinerariifolium*. It affects the nervous system of cold-blooded creatures like insects. Use it sparingly as it also affects fish, spiders, ladybirds and other useful insects. It does not affect bees. Pyrethrum preparations can be obtained in the garden trade as sprays or misting agents.

Warning: Pyrethrum preparations can be highly toxic to humans if they penetrate open wounds, broken skin or the blood stream. Also strictly avoid inhaling misted spray.

Chemical control should really be a last resort if other methods have failed or if infestation has reached epidemic proportions. You can obtain preparations from the gardening trade which can be sprayed, watered, dusted on or in the form of sticks that are pushed into the compost.
● Insecticides are effective against biting and sucking insects but also affect useful insects.

● Acaricides kill off mites.
● Fungicides are effective against fungal diseases.

Rules when handling plant protection agents
● Do not use highly toxic preparations.
● If you use sprays, you should only use those that do not contain CFCs in order to protect the environment.
● Adhere strictly to the manufacturer's instructions for use and dosage. Keep to the spraying intervals indicated so that subsequent generations of pests are also destroyed.
● Only ever prepare as much of a solution for spraying as you are actually going to use. Remains of spray and out of date preparations should be disposed of with dangerous waste (ask your local council).
● Always wear rubber gloves when handling toxic preparations.
● Only use or spray substances that are lethal for bees in very exceptional cases and only late in the evening.
● Do not spray on windy days and make sure that the spray mist does not drift on to a neighbour's balcony or windowsill nor run down on to the street.
● Never spray in bright sunlight or when it is raining. The best times are on slightly overcast, calm days.
● Never inhale the spray mist.
● Always store the protection agent in its original packaging, out of reach of children and pets, never together with food or animal feed and locked away.

Diseases

Fungal diseases
Prevention
● Air the winter quarters of your plants daily even in cold weather.
● On cool, overcast days, carefully water the plants outside or in winter quarters, making sure that only the rootstocks are touched by the water. Any water on the leaves will dry off very slowly on cold days and thus encourage infestation by fungi.
● Water in the mornings so that moist leaves can dry off by evening.
● Stand your plants in loose groups with enough space between them so that the air can circulate freely. Standing them too close together will encourage fungal infection.
● As a prevention, water or spray your plants with ready-made preparations (from the garden trade) in the spring and summer to fortify them against fungi, or use home-made brews containing comfrey, nettle, yarrow or mare's tail.
Control: Carefully remove infested parts of the plant so that healthy leaves do not become contaminated and infected with dust or fungal spores.
● To combat mildew, spray with mare's tail brew or garlic tea.
● Rust can also be treated with a spray of garlic tea.
● Sooty mould is caused by infestation by aphids and white fly whose sticky, honeydew secretions are colonized by the fungus. Remove badly infested parts and wash off other parts with tepid water.

The five most common diseases

Bacterial blight (*Xanthomonas pelargonii*) – Symptoms: black discoloration and decay of the base of the stem. Brown red to yellow green spots on the leaves. The plant stems snap and die.
Cause: bacterial infection through contaminated soil or using a dirty knife when taking cuttings.
Remedy: see bacterial infections, page 59.

Downy mildew – Symptoms: a colony of whitish-grey fungus on the undersides of leaves. Pale yellow spots that turn darker on the top sides of leaves. Later, drying out and death of the leaves.
Cause: fungus spores, encouraged by high humidity and lack of circulating air.
Remedy: see fungal diseases (left).

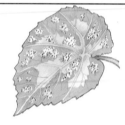

Powdery mildew – Symptoms: a mealy film (that can be washed off) on the leaves (undersides and tops) and stems. At an advanced stage, the leaves look crippled and warped.
Cause: fungal spores encouraged by temperature fluctuations as well as wet leaves in cool, wet weather.
Remedy: see fungal diseases (left).

Rust – Symptoms: red brown to dark brown blisters on the leaves and stems. Infested parts die off.
Cause: fungal spores, encouraged by high humidity and warm weather. Remains of water or rain on the leaves along with cool weather.
Remedy: see fungal diseases (left).

Sooty mould – Symptoms: black, sticky substance on leaves, stems and shoot tips.
Cause: colonies of sooty mould fungus on the honeydew secretions of aphids, scale insects and mealy bugs.
Remedy: controlling the aphids (see pests, p. 59).

Bacterial inefections

Prevention: Make sure plants are healthy when you buy them. Always disinfect your knife with alcohol when taking cuttings and use germ-free compost.

Control: It is not possible to cure the plant, only to extend its life. Immediately remove infested leaves and shoots and dust the cut surfaces with charcoal powder. Do not take cuttings from these plants and do not throw them on the compost heap from where infection may spread to other plants, but destroy them.

Pests

Prevention

● Protect plants from draughts and dryness.

● Fertilize the plants regularly but do not overdo things. Too much nitrogen will make the leaves grow too large and the tissue will be soft and spongy – just the sort of snack loved by all pests. Too much nitrogen will also prevent the formation of flowers.

● Regularly remove weeds from troughs and boxes as they will encourage pests.

Control

● Spray with garlic tea to combat spider mites. Spraying the plants several times will help with a mild infestation.

● For aphids and white fly, spray fermented nettle brew, nettle extract or soap solution

● Scratch off scale insects and clean the parts of the plant with a moist, warm cloth. Spray with a paraffin oil preparation or soap solution.

● Green capsids can be picked off. Pyrethrum preparations should only be used for a severe infestation.

The five most common pests

Aphids – Symptoms: crinkled, rolled up and warped leaves and shoots. Colonies of green, red or black aphids on the undersides of leaves. The leaves are sticky.
Cause: infestation encouraged by dry air, warmth and over-fertilizing.
Remedy: see pest control (left).

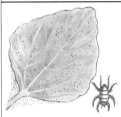

Red spider mites – Symptoms: fine webs with reddish or green yellow mites on the undersides of leaves. Whitish-yellow spots on the uppersides of leaves. The leaves turn pale, dry up and die off.
Cause: infestation is encouraged by a dry/warm climate and stagnant air.
Remedy: see pest control (left).

Scale insects – Symptoms: small, brown knobs and lumps on the leaves and stems, which are easy to scratch off. Sticky leaves (secretions of the insects) which are colonized by sooty mould.
Cause: infestation due to overwintering in a warm place.
Remedy: see pest control (left).

White fly – Symptoms: white, flying insect and green larvae on the undersides of the leaves. When the leaves are touched, the insects fly up in a small cloud. Sticky leaves.
Cause: dry air, warmth. The insect occurs primarily in greenhouses.
Remedy: see pest control (left).

(Green capsid) – Symptoms: crippled leaves with holes, flowerbuds and shoot tips with perforations that turn brown.
Cause: the pests suck the plants' sap in dry, hot weather.
Remedy: see pest control (left).

Index

Index

Index

Addresses

Rare seeds
Thompson & Morgan,
London Road, Ipswich,
Suffolk IP2 OBA

Author's note
This guide deals with the positioning, arrangement and care of balcony plants as well as ornamental trees, shrubs, grasses and bulbs which are grown in containers. It is important to place these containers on the balcony or fix them to a windowsill in such a way that they are secure and cannot fall down even in high winds (see pp. 13 and 14/15). In addition, always place a saucer or bowl under each container to catch any excess water and to prevent water from running on to a neighbour's balcony or down on to the street below.

Some of the plants described here are very toxic, others contain skin irritants or allergy-provoking substances. All such plants have been indicated with a warning symbol in the tables on pages 20/21 and an explicit warning in the section on arranging. Please make absolutely sure that children and pets cannot eat any parts of these plants, otherwise considerable health problems may result. If you suffer from contact allergies, you should put on gloves before touching these plants.

While sowing and planting balcony plants, you will come into contact with soil and compost. If you suffer any injuries while handling these substances, you should consult a doctor and get professional treatment. Discuss the possibility of having a tetanus vaccination. Fertilizers and plant protection agents should always be stored in a place that is inaccessible to children and animals. If you use chemical plant protection agents, do so only on windless days and when your immediate neighbours are not on their balconies. Wear gloves and do not inhale the spray mist (see p. 57).

A box for summer and autumn
(see photo inside back cover)
This arrangement will give you delicate flowers during the summer and interesting seedheads in the autumn.

Plants for a 60-cm (24 in) box:
baby blue eyes, *Nemophila menziesii* (light blue)
convolvulus, *Convolvulus sabatius* (light blue)
Cape marigold, *Dimorphotheca sinuata* (cream, yellow, orange)
quaking grass, *Briza minor* (green)
Asperula orientalis (light blue)
toadflax, *Linaria maroccana* (white, yellow, red, blue)
blue sage, *Salvia patens* (cobalt blue)
Californian poppy, *Eschscholzia californica* (cream, yellow, orange, red)
abutilon, *Abutilon megapotamicum* (yellow, red)

Planting and care: The convolvulus and abutilon can be bought in the spring; all the other plants can be pre-grown in trays etc. in late spring and planted in the box when ready.

Alternative: sow directly in the box during the last month of spring and, if too many seeds germinate, thin them out. The convolvulus and the abutilon can be overwintered inside; the others are annuals.

Cover photographs
Front cover: *A summer box with black-eyed Susan, yellow marigolds, red pelargoniums, violet petunias and convolvulus (see p. 29).*
Inside front cover: *Nemesia (Nemesia hybrid).*
Inside back cover: *A box for summer and autumn (see p. 63).*
Back cover: *Amphora with pockets filled with busy lizzie (Impatiens walleriana hybrids) and various varieties of ivy.*

Photographic acknowledgements
Becherer: p. 8;
Silvestris/Layer: p. 22;
Strauss: all other photographs. The photographer also arranged all the plantings on balconies and in boxes on pp. 4/4, 11, 12, 19, 23, 25 bottom left, 29, 39, 45, 48/49, 50, 53, 56.

Artwork acknowledgements
Marlene Gemke: pp. 14, 15, 54, 55;
Ushie Dorner: pp. 58, 59;
György Jankovics: pp. 20, 21 (symbols)

This edition published 1995 by
Merehurst Limited
Ferry House, 51-57 Lacy Road,
Putney, London SW15 1PR

© 1992 Gräfe und Unzer GmbH, Munich

ISBN 1 85391 443 6

English text copyright ©
Merehurst Limited 1994
Translated by Astrid Mick
Edited by Lesley Young
Design and typesetting by Paul Cooper
Printed in Singapore by Craft Print Pte Ltd